Tears of Sorrow, Tears of Joy

*Stories and Lessons
of a Grace-Filled Life*

Stan Goss

K. Lynn Lewis, *Managing Editor*
Hannah Menslage, *Developmental Editor*

EQUIP PEOPLE FOR HIS GOOD WORKS

Katy, Texas

Copyright © 2023 Stan Goss

ALL RIGHTS RESERVED. No part of this publication may be reproduced, stored in, or introduced into a retrieval system, or transmitted in any form or by any means (electronic, mechanical, photocopying, recording, or otherwise) without prior written permission.

This work includes personal reflections and opinions by the author for informational and inspirational purposes only. Statistics, Internet web sites, and digital content referenced may have changed or disappeared between the time of research and writing and the time of reading.

Print ISBN: 979-8-9858296-4-8
Digital ISBN: 979-8-9858296-5-5
Library of Congress Control Number: 2023952345

Original cover photos and most interior photos provided by Stan Goss. Cover graphic design, interior layout and graphics, and redwood tree photo (p. 74) by K. Lynn Lewis. Waldo Leggett photo (p. 60) by Stephanie Leggett. Organizational logos selected from official publications.

Developmental editing by Hannah Menslage of WordSword.

Unless otherwise noted, Scripture quotations are taken from the Holy Bible, English Standard Version. ESV® Text Edition: 2016. Copyright © 2001 by Crossway Bibles, a publishing ministry of Good News Publishers.

Those marked "NIV" are taken from the Holy Bible, New International Version®, NIV®. Copyright © 1973, 1978, 1984 by Biblica, Inc.™ Used by permission of Zondervan. All rights reserved worldwide. Zondervan.com.

Excerpts of writings published in Wake-Up Call on Seedbed.com are used with permission from the author, J.D. Walt.

Published by Nehemiah Press
NehemiahPress.com
Katy, Texas

TESTIMONIALS

"Have you ever met a person who gives you advice without saying a word, without writing a word? Have you ever been around a leader who puts those who follow that leadership ahead of himself and sacrifices for those who follow? Have you found a person who clearly follows Jesus? Have you ever met a person who listens so well that you really do not need to explain what you mean by what you have said? Have you ever known someone who you wanted to be your personal coach because you knew that you would grow in your business? Have you discovered a person whose example you might follow, and if you did, you would have confidence you were going in the right direction? I have! Stan Goss."

Thom Polvogt, Author, and Vice-President of Caleb Insurance Group

"Stan Goss has lived a rich life filled with challenges, suffering, and blessings. Stan is a faithful witness to God's presence, love, mercy, and grace, available to all who accept Jesus Christ as their Lord and Savior. I am blessed that Stan and I are friends."

Richard Selke, Disciple maker

"I love Stan. Stan is more than a friend; he is a brother! Though I haven't known Stan most of my life, I wish I had. Not because of his successes in the business world of executive coaching and other ventures in life, but rather because he loves deeply! He loves Jesus and others to the core. He embodies Titus 2. I deeply cherish our relationship. The art of wisdom being passed down relationally is lost on this generation who is enamored with the 'new.' However, in Titus 2 we see that God designed us to learn from each other; the young from the older and wiser, and old from the passionate, dreaming younger. Stan's life embodies this. Good experiences and bad ones, Stan isn't afraid to share it all in his book. I am wiser and better for knowing him."

Jeff Dietz, Campus Pastor at Grace Fellowship Church

"I met Stan many years ago when he invited me to join a morning men's study that emphasized a Spirit-led life. Stan was a recognized leader in our community who had used his secular skills to have a positive impact with men, particularly corporate leaders, and those who were open to new direction in their lives. As we studied and openly shared, a transformation began taking place within our own lives; this was openly shared by Stan. He saw the grace of our Lord in his own life, and recognized it as the Spirit of Jesus, using his life experiences to transform him and others. A true leader sets the example for others who, through the crucible of fire, follow the Holy Spirit in ministry and learn that all of life's experiences can have a positive impact. Stan Goss is such a leader, and by God's grace, his love for others is now fully Spirit-led."

Ron Dagley, Retired Commercial Real Estate Executive

"Stan Goss is a beacon of enduring faith and a testament to the power of God's grace. Throughout my friendship with Stan, I have learned that in every chapter of his life, he has exemplified unwavering devotion, teaching, and inspiring countless souls, myself included. His journey, as shared in 'Tears of Sorrow, Tears of Joy,' is not just his own, but a shared reflection of the many lives he has touched. I've been privileged to witness some of these stories firsthand, and they've always served as profound reminders of God's ever-present love and guidance. As one of the Godliest men I have had the honor to know, Stan's tales are not just lessons, but true treasures of a life lived in close communication with our Father above."

Don McCoy, President/CEO of the Fulshear-Katy Area Chamber of Commerce

"Stan Goss, my friend, is a man among men; he is a coach of coaches. Ever since I met him, I've observed him walk in a perpetual 'thin space,' where Heaven and Earth are so closely connected in his life that he cannot help but stand near the Lord. His reliance on the Holy Spirit has provided him with so much inner love, joy, peace, patience, kindness, goodness, faithfulness, gentleness, and self-control that he makes the Gospel attractive to others. I am refreshed every time I see him because he helps me believe that I, too, can live out the 'fruit of the Spirit.' His constant obedience has continuously blessed him and his family, and in turn, it has radiated to countless others, including myself. Thank God for Stan Goss."

David "Coach" Nelson, Men's Ministry Pastor at Real Life Ministries Texas

"I have known Stan for many years now, and one thing I can say is that his words are lived out. How Stan has chosen to live his life, in spite of his tragic childhood upbringing, has brought healing and guidance to countless people as he has lived out Romans 8:28, 'And we know that for those who love God all things work together for good, for those who are called according to his purpose.' Stan's intentional life-giving fellowship points people toward Jesus and seeks God's best for your life. Stan is willing to walk alongside you with wisdom and encouragement to help you on your journey. He leads a life well lived and worthy of your time to read."

Chuck Nelson, President of Steadfast Construction Services

"Stan Goss has been my executive coach, spiritual mentor, and dear friend for many years. From the moment I met Stan, I knew there was something different about him. He was so full of grace, patience, wisdom, and strength. As I learned his life's story, it became clear to me that the energy I saw within him was not from Stan himself, but derived from God, working through the Holy Spirit. The stories you will soon read in this book and the wisdom you will take away are truly inspired by the Holy Spirit. Stan is a man who deeply understands his place with God is only through Jesus Christ, our Lord and Savior."

Bob Chalker, Retired Chief Executive at AAMP

"Stan Goss is an insightful, informed, and wise person who has always looked to the future with dreams and a strong desire to serve. He has been a fearless warrior to help men and women connect with their God and Lord, Jesus Christ. In a world that is increasingly anti-Christian, Stan lives each day with one purpose: to bring those he meets to the Lord.

Our forty years of personal and professional friendship have been a blessing to me, and I thank God that our paths crossed. May Stan continue to inspire those he meets with joy and love like he did me so many years ago."

    Deacon Randy Graham, Director of Family Life at St. Faustina Catholic Church

"I came to know Stan through his efforts with the Men's Ministry in the Katy area. His insight into how God has forged men helped me grow in both my faith and my abilities to relate to my wife, my children, and others. Later, I got to know Stan much deeper through the Colson Fellows Program, a year-long study of the biblical worldview and how to apply it to the craziness around us. Stan came prepared for each session, providing wisdom he'd obtained through many years of experiences. His book will provide us all with a great opportunity to reap the benefits of those wisdoms."

    Kip Thompson, Colson Fellows graduate and a small group leader at Grace Fellowship Church

"Stan Goss is one of the most loving and genuinely authentic people I've ever had the pleasure of knowing. He is a tremendous influence in my life as a teacher, mentor, truth-teller, and spiritual guide. Stan has amazing insights to see and know the blessings of life, and to share them from a place of love and compassion. I am a far better man, father, and friend to the people in my life thanks to my relationship with Stan. Truly one of God's precious gifts."

    Terry Krailo, Vice-President of Marketing & Graphic Communications at Baylor College of Medicine

"I first met Stan over ten years ago when I joined the Katy Area Economic Development Council. Stan not only became my friend, but an enlightening mentor who changed my business life and most crucially, my relationship with Jesus. He taught me the true meaning of being Christ-like in all of life's relationships. I've had quite the ride with Sir Stan, and I can't even begin to wonder where my life would be without his dynamic influence. I love Stan and look forward to many more years of friendship and good times."

    Paul Kurt, President of Kurt and Associates and Chairman of the Board of Governors at the Katy Area Economic Development Council

"I've had the privilege of doing life with Stan Goss for the past decade. Stan is my small group leader, my mentor and discipler, a wise friend and a sage, and an inspiration who models how to live a Spirit-filled life. Stan has allowed me to discover that there truly is no retirement in God's kingdom, and that my best days of loving, living, and serving Jesus are in front of me. The tales of God's grace throughout Stan's book will help you realize the hand and purpose of God in your daily life and will empower you to live life to the fullest through Christ. Enjoy and be filled from the life wisdom of my friend and brother, Stan Goss."

    Rev. Dr. Blair Lerner, Spiritual Formation & Outreach Director at Grace Fellowship Church

"If you are looking for an inspirational life story, this one is a story of redemption and grace. Stan's seemingly never-ending pursuit of personal growth and deepening relationship with God is inspiring. He has impacted countless lives as he has worked with men to find healing

from the things that keeps them from being all God called them to be. What is most amazing to me is that his story is still being written. God's not done with him yet. I am so thankful that Stan has shared his experience of grace (up to this point), and I am looking forward to see what God and Stan do next.

Roy Wooten, Executive Director of The Crucible Project

CONTENTS

Love Letters		xi
Preface		xv
1.	Men Don't Cry	1
2.	Memoirs of Grace: How Unimaginable Tragedies Shaped My Life	3
3.	From Verbal to Written: How God's Grace Got the Words on the Page	25
4.	Demographic Realities of an Aging Population	27
5.	I've Had 62 Jobs, but I'd Always Wanted to be a Coach	33
6.	How a Talented but Difficult Executive Helped Me Launch My Executive Coaching Career	37
7.	Growing Clarity and Awareness of "The Answers Within"	45
8.	From Focus on the World to Focus on the Word	47
9.	On the Invisibility of Aging	49
10.	Along Comes Colson	53
11.	Finishing Well with Grace	55
12.	Men's Work and God's Perfect Plan	63
13.	My Father's Ring, My Father's Blessing, and Tears of Joy	69
14.	Moving on With Men	73
15.	All Roads Lead to the Sad State of Modern Men	75
16.	Initiating Men into a New Way of Manhood	77
17.	My "Romeo Group" and What They Have Meant to Me	83
18.	"Wake-Up Call," Formerly Known as "The Daily Seedbed Text," and J.D. Walt	85
19.	Crown of Glory: A Manifesto for Christian Spiritual Eldership	87

20.	God: The Great Dot Connector	91
21.	It Only Took 82 Years of Being a Christian to Reach a Complete Understanding of the Holy Spirit of Jesus in Me	95
22.	Awakened Wedding Vows	97
23.	From Practical Atheism to Spirit-Filled Christian Spiritual Eldership	105
24.	'Signals of Transcendence' in a World of Practical Atheism	107
25.	How Now Shall We Live Out Our Crown of Glory Years?	111
26.	Complete Your Understanding of the Holy Spirit and Embody the Transformation Within	113
27.	Prepare for Training	115
28.	Have the End in Mind	117
29.	Your Life IS Your Ministry	119
30.	Why It's Time for You to Enter the Ministry	121
31.	Starting Over With Grace	125
32.	Grace, a State of "Bee-ing"	129
33.	Age, Eldership, and the Sage	141
34.	How Sowing Seeds Builds the Kingdom of God	145
35.	Disturb the System, Make Waves, Be Bold and Fear Not	153
36.	The Sword of Truth	159
37.	See the Sacred in the Everyday Rituals of Life	161
38.	Taking It All to the Next Level	165

Appendix	169
Syllabus	173
About the Author	179

LOVE LETTERS

I've chosen to title this typical "Acknowledgements" section "Love Letters."

With eighty-five years of a splendidly grace-filled life, my love letters could easily include hundreds of souls I've encountered who have blessed, inspired, healed, and encouraged me. They have shown me the way, given me joy, wiped my tears, reached out in difficult times, taught me lessons, learned from me, and had open arms, open minds, and open hearts.

Yet for the purpose of this book, I've been forced to shorten this list.

First and foremost, I want to thank my soulmate, my creative genius, my increasingly in-sync partner, as we've grown old together, with laughs, light, and love. This beloved soul is Suzi Q – my wife, my queen, my wise woman, and my best friend.

Secondly, I want to thank my precious family. Some are close, some not. I miss the ones gone or lost and cherish the ones present. I'll place their names simply alphabetically, and you all will get letters from heaven!

Chris, David, Heather, Lisa, Steve, and Tim, and the best daughters-in-love ever, Jackie and Sarah.

Next, the grandchildren. You make all the good things they say about grandkids ring true. In alphabetical order, because you are all my favorites: Alison (Ice Water), Brant (and Jen), Drew, Emily, Jordan, Michaela (and Mac), Sarah (Money) and Zach.

To the rest of my beloved family, I could write a whole separate book. We have shared many adventures, memories, rituals, virtues, and trips – many tears, much joy; much heartbreak, much healing; and so many games, circles, gatherings, and check-ins.

To my New Warrior Band of Brothers: What a crew we were! I write to Tom Hopwood, Al Levi (RIP), Gene Perry, Alastair Livingston, Paul Gilford, Steve Beach, Ken Rogers (RIP), and Bill McNinch (RIP).

To my Warrior mentors and teachers: David Lindgren, Joe Lauer, Rich Tosi (RIP), and Ron Hering (RIP). You each identified something within me that I didn't realize I had. You reached out, fostered this, and never let go!

And to my partners, the best partners I've ever had: Bubby Levy (RIP), Kevin O'Brien (RIP), and Terry Krailo.

To my fellow sages: Lindell West, Thom Polvogt, Richard Selke, Blair Lerner, Ron Dagley, Neil Hurd, Mike Lejeuene, George Sayre, and Glenn Smith.

To my Golf Guys: Ron Dagley, Paul Vanek, and Downey Vickery... AHO! Thank you all for bringing me along for the ride and giving me the "unfair advantage" in God's great outdoor playground!

Of course, I want to thank to my wise women, as no man's life can be complete without the presence of wise women: Jeanine Baker, Margaret McNinch, Pat Strobel, Cheryl Bryan, Wynette Stuntz, Margie Seaman, Susan Coulter, Karen McCullough, and Suzi Goss.

To my inspirational pastors and teachers: Paul Helbig, Jim Leggett, Blair Lerner, Jeff Dietz, J.D. Walt, and Paul Saavedra.

To my Colson Compadres: Kip Thomson, for your steadfast purpose; and Andy Johnston, Angel Pennyman, and Carmen Carter for staying in touch and keeping the faith.

To The Bible Seminary: Thank you Lynn Lewis, for all you do; and Mickey Williamson Ellis and Alison Taylor for your encouragement and coaching.

To my Crucible Brother Redwoods: Roy Wooten and David Nelson.

To my clients-turned-friends and then brothers: Bob Chalker, Art Shelton, Lance LaCour, Randy Limbacher, Ron Schwarz, Paul Kurt, Jeff Moseley, Jody Batdorf, and Randy Graham.

To my neighbors: You have each made our neighborhood a living, breathing manifestation of the call to "love your neighbor."

To my newfound sources of light, energy, and faith in action: Joseph Menslage, Erica Scardino, Jay Donella, Pernell Hill, and Jason Hall.

To the one who has been my co-creative partner in bringing this book to life: Hannah Menslage of WordSword. Without your vision, encouragement, unique skills, and genius, this book would never have materialized!

And primarily, all thanks and glory to my Lord and Savior, Jesus Christ!

PREFACE

How Now Shall We Live Our Glory Years?

If the good Lord wills it, and the publishing process favors me, by the time this book meets your hands, I will be eighty-five years old. This will be my first book.

Throughout the past thirty years or so, people have told me that I should write a book. I have made several futile attempts to do so yet have always fallen short. I even engaged some brilliant writing muses to help. The result was the same; I never quite got a book out of it. Some good articles, certainly, but no book.

Naturally, I have read several books about writing, all offering similar advice, "If you want to write, pick up a pen and write." Still, I didn't produce much for a long time.

Some time ago, I was honored by the Carl Jung Center in Houston as their *Man of the Year* for my years-long work with men. The Gala turned out a large crowd, and for the evening, I sat at the head table next to the keynote speaker. He was a man named Sam Keen, a prolific writer on men's issues, with a bestselling classic, *Fire in the Belly: On Being a Man* (Bantam, 1992).

I shared with him my admiration for his work and confided in him my mental barrier in completing my own book. His response imitated what I'd heard for years, "The secret to writing is to write." Then, he acknowledged my personal gift, which was the basis for my award: the ability to build community.

Finally, I share with you my journey. Some of the most significant memories of my voyage, which carried me to this eighty-fifth year milestone, begin around the time I was eight years old. The space between eight and eighty-five is the basis for this book.

Stan Goss
Tuesday, April 25, 2023

Chapter 1
Men Don't Cry

I have cried most of my life. I was never quite sure why my tears flowed so willingly. I recall crying after a tough loss as a fresh-faced high school athlete and coaches telling me: "Men don't cry."

I grew up a diehard Denver Broncos fan. In the 90s, when John Elway led them to their first and second Super Bowl victories, I cried.

Later, when Elway announced his retirement on ESPN, he cried. He tried not to but couldn't hold back his tears. And from my television set worlds away, I cried with him. What great years he provided for his fans!

The next day, wearing my Broncos hat in line at the grocery store, the lady cashier noted my hat and asked if I had seen Elway on TV the night before. I told her I did, to which she responded, "He cried. I hate it when men cry."

I replied, "I cried too. After all, men are human!"

Later in life, I finally learned my tears: some tears of sorrow, some tears of joy. And over the years, many men told me that through my own tears, I showed them how to feel.

My first vivid memory of crying was at my father's funeral. As they closed the lid on his casket, the pastor paused to ask me if I wanted my father's ring. To this, my small face erupted into deep grief and sorrow, and I wept, "No, let him keep it. It is his."

I carried my burden of tears well into my adult years, crying my way through life. But redemption finally came in a very surprising way through my Father's Ring.

But first, a story...

Chapter 2
Memoirs of Grace: How Unimaginable Tragedies Shaped My Life

Nancy. I've never remembered much about her. She was my only sibling and a few years younger than me. Our lives as young children did produce a few beautiful images that remain in my memory. I do know that she was a very talented dancer; there is ample evidence of that in the old photos. She was cute with elegant, long legs.

Probably my last photos of her were taken when she was around fourteen or fifteen years old. I also have a handful of baby pictures of a cute little black-haired, button-nosed girl who was obviously my sister, Nancy.

Nonetheless, I have few other memories, equivocally good or bad, which I suppose is evidence that God gives us just about what we can handle.

I once spoke with a forty-nine-year-old friend deeply grieving over the premature loss of her husband. A forty-nine-year-old minister on a mission trip to a mountainous region of Africa, he died of altitude sickness before they could get medical help.

He left her with two children, adopted teens, who were having difficulty dealing with the loss of their dad. She was in a tough place emotionally.

During our conversation, I shared the story of my own family losses. Her response was that, in a way, I was lucky to have experienced all those losses early in life and did not have to deal with them as an adult. She compared me to Benjamin Button, and in many ways, I think she is right. I did have to do a lot of heavy lifting early in life. And I have felt, for several years, that I was getting younger.

But more about that later.

My family lived on a wheat farm in eastern Colorado, a few miles outside of the tiny town of Bennett. The town hosted a population of 200, plus or minus a bit. We moved there from Austin, Texas, when I was around six years old. My mom, dad, baby sister Nancy, and I went to live on the farm with my grandparents, Oscar and Beatrice. I never knew why we moved there, although in adulthood, I've speculated that it was because World War II was waging. I do remember that I enjoyed living there very much. I had my own horse, Trigger, whom I rode everywhere, including to school when the school bus path was obstructed by the snowy winter roads.

Our school consisted of four modest classrooms that hosted grades 1-12, with each room serving three grades. We also had a barn and a gym. Basketball was big in our region, because most of the surrounding schools, like Strasburg, Agate and Deer Trail, didn't have enough high school-aged boys for other sports. This is doubtlessly where my lifelong love for basketball originated. Bennett Tigers, black and orange. Orange is still my favorite color. Just ask any of my grandkids!

I learned the essential nature of a strong work ethic on the farm. Farm life consists of endless work, and kids lend hands out of necessity. I herded cows on my horse, Trigger. During harvest time, I milked all the cows, perhaps forty or so. I also drove the pickup truck, running errands during harvest time. I had my own Holstein calf, Dottie, and my own pig that I caught at the Arapahoe County Fair. She was a black and white, Poland China sow with a big white band that circled her belly. I named her Bijou Echo III. Later, I had Bijou bred and donated one of her babies back into the fair's "Catch-It" contest. That was part of the deal. I guess the rest of her litter became pork chops, ham, and bacon.

I retain many fond memories of farm life. Small snippets circle my mind, appearing here and there. Time, however, is an interesting construct, and questions arise about which memories were real, and which were imagined. The problem lies in that nobody remains who could confirm or deny most of my fragments.

Yet, my darker memories have led me to the astonishing conclusion to this story. I have told this part many times and done a lot of personal, healing "inner work" as a result. And I have cried countless tears over it. But until recently, I never wrote it down.

A Really Bad Season

A lot of what I'm about to reveal is surreal. I know it happened. I'm never quite sure I have every detail right. All who could confirm them are long gone. That is why the last part of this story is so crucial.

I remember myself as a youngster riding in the passenger seat of our pick-up truck with my father at steering the wheel. We were following my uncle Grady, who was driving a flat-bed truck with a tractor chained to the flatbed. Right in front of our eyes, he drove off the road into a ditch and the tractor broke loose and pinned him in the cab. The scene was horrific. My dad left me alone with Uncle Grady to search desperately for help. Pools of blood remain ingrained in my memory. These, and that Uncle Grady died. I think he was thirty-something. That's all I remember.

OSCAR LANKFORD

Sometime thereafter, I was out fishing with my grandpa, Oscar Lankford. My memories of him, along with the pictures I have seen, depict him as a tall, quiet man. He was sort of the "Gregory Peck" type. Yet on this day, my memories become fuzzy. My grandpa had a heart attack and died. The story is that I dragged his body into the pickup truck and drove to the nearest farm for help.

That's one perquisite of being a farm kid. You learn to drive early. Country terrain is endlessly turning land, dirt trails and roads with no traffic. This comes in handy during harvest time, or fence building, or when your grandpa dies, and you need to search for help. I don't recall a funeral, grieving, or anything. Zip. Nada. Perhaps God just gives us what we can handle, and He takes care of the rest.

The nightmare continued when my dad, Claude Benton Goss, died a few weeks later. We were alone on the tractor night plowing. I think he had a heart attack. I do remember my mom yelling at him to wake up. He didn't. I remember an ambulance driving away with his body, and that was it.

A Fresh Start in Aurora, Colorado

Sometime afterwards, we pulled down the driveway of the farm and moved into the city, Aurora, a suburb of Denver. My mom needed work and she took me along. I spent the rest of my upbringing there with just my mom and me. Little Nancy, older now, stayed back on the farm with my grandma.

My remaining junior high and high school years were spent in Aurora. These I look back on as really good years. I always had jobs sacking groceries, throwing newspapers, and so on. I made my own money and my "good old farm boy" work ethic proved handy. I was also a straight-A student and an excellent athlete. I loved sports, particularly basketball, and practically slept with a basketball cradled in my arms.

But life in Aurora wasn't without problems. My mother started to drink. It wasn't until years later, retrospectively, that I realized the incredible pain she must have felt with the loss of her husband, brother, and father. At the time, I was only a kid, striving to be her hero-man child. And I did my best with that, but I couldn't save her from her alcoholic pain.

A teenage caretaker of an alcoholic mother is hard work. I do have some vivid memories of this that I have successfully buried out of sight. Still, I navigated life as well as I could and performed well enough in school that I ended up gaining admission into a couple of excellent colleges. I earned an appointment with the U.S Naval Academy and a full-ride scholarship to the Colorado School of Mines in Golden, Colorado. I opted to attend the School of Mines, the top school in the world for earth sciences engineering in the fields of petroleum engineering, mining, geophysics, and metallurgy.

I studied at Mines for two-and-a-half years. My grades were decent, but it became clear to me that engineering wasn't what I wanted to do with my life. The highlights of my time at Mines involved sports. As a freshman, I remained undefeated at the varsity level in track in the 880-yard (half-mile) run, and I won the conference championship. I also made the varsity basketball team as a freshman and sophomore.

In the half mile, the Miners dominated both first and second places. Stan Goss and Bob Pearson beat out Bollie Bell in the half mile, winning with a 2:07.4 time.	Excerpt from "Colorado Mines Clips Bear Track Team Here," *Greeley Tribune*, Thursday, April 18, 1957, p. 12.

A Change of Plans

Then, one monumental event changed my life at Mines. I married my high school sweetheart, Christine Webb. Christine, or Tina, as she was called, was two years my junior in school. She completed high school in Kansas City, and upon graduation, moved back to Denver to live with her sister. She and I had dated steadily, and in my college years we decided to get married and start a family.

I abruptly dropped out of school and got a job with the Colorado Department of Highways where I had previously worked many summers. Tina and I became teenage parents, desperately trying to pave our way in life with little guidance or help. This dealt a crushing blow to my mom. When I left home for college, Nancy moved from the farm – where she lived during my high-school years – to live with our mother in Aurora. She was in junior high school.

Much of my recollection of those years has been lost within my mind's abyss. From what I've managed to retain, when I left college and moved back to Aurora, I was more aware than ever of our mother's drinking problem. I find glimpses of grim memories, including nights where I'd tried to host failed "interventions." This would be heavy to handle at any age, and I will never forget how helpless I felt.

My decision to leave college ruined her dreams for me. I'm sure she blamed my then-wife. My mother openly resented Tina, and their relationship was always rocky. And little Nancy, I'm sure she had endured many similar struggles. But Nancy had found an outlet in her dancing. She was an incredibly talented dancer and earned many awards.

Another Dark Day

Many events conspired to bring me into the next dark day of my life. I was working one morning when the phone rang for me. My mom greeted me urgently, informing me that both she and Nancy had the flu.

"Could you call in sick for us?" she asked.

I agreed and phoned my mother's work and Nancy's school. I then raced to the house, checked in on them, and fixed them a bite to eat. They were sick, but seemed stable, so I returned to work.

A few hours passed. Later that afternoon, I called the house and received no answer. I assumed my mom and Nancy were feeling better and read this as a positive omen, imagining perhaps they stepped out to shop.

I had felt a bit sick when I returned to work earlier, but recovered quickly, so I supposed the same was true for them. I made a mental promise to return to the house after work to check on them. Yet when "after work" arrived, I remembered that I had promised Tina that I would take her shopping and did that instead.

Later, when we arrived home, the phone was blaring. I answered it only to hear a neighbor's frantic voice urging me to rush to the house. I arrived within minutes to a sea of flashing red lights and several emergency vehicles. When I stepped inside, I saw my mother's limp body on the floor and a gurney was wheeling Nancy outside and into an ambulance. It was all a blur after that.

I know that someone directed me inside the ambulance with Nancy, and that I spent the night alone at the hospital as people worked feverishly to save her life.

But Nancy didn't make it. She was only fifteen years old.

Authorities determined that the house was flooded with carbon monoxide gas. Evidently, my mother pulled a panel off the furnace that kept the gas from recycling into the house. Without this panel in place, the house became a lethal gas chamber. We never knew how or why this happened.

I have few memories of their funeral. Many showed up, including people from Nancy's school, which let them out to attend. I remember the procession from the funeral to the cemetery seemed to stretch for miles. They were both buried close to my dad, and I have only returned a couple of times.

Tears of Sorrow, Tears of Joy

Faulty Furnace Kills Local Mother, Daughter

NANCY GOSS

MRS. RUTH O. GOSS

A faulty furnace has been blamed for the tragic carbon monoxide deaths of Mrs. Ruth O. Goss, 52, and her daughter Nancy, 15, this week according to reports by the Aurora Police Department.

Mrs. Goss, who lived at 1386 Geneva Street, called her son, Stanley Goss, 21, 528 Marion, Denver, about 8:30 a.m. Monday morning saying she was not feeling well and asked him to have his wife Christine notify the Chemical Sales Company that she would not be to work.

Stan drove to his mother's home to find that his sister was also ill. Mrs. Goss surmised that they were coming down with the flu and would both stay home to recuperate. About 9:30 a.m. Stan Goss left his mother and sister, after fixing them tea and toast, and went on to work at the State Highway Department.

Monday evening alarmed neighbors called Dr. Eugene Penn to the home. Dr. Penn found Mrs. Goss dead on the living room floor and Nancy in her bed unconscious. Nancy was taken to Colorado General Hospital by the Aurora-Chase Ambulance where doctors worked for 15 hours to save her life. She passed away at 12:12 Tuesday afternoon.

Mrs. Goss was employed by the Aurora Advocate about a year ago. Her husband, Claude, died of a heart attack when the family resided in Bennett, Colorado, in 1950. It was following his death that they moved to Aurora. She will be laid to rest next to her husband at Fairmount Cemetery.

Nancy was a student at West Junior High School and active in the Aurora Assembly #53, Rainbow Girls.

Double funeral rites will be said by Dr. J. Carlton Babbs, pastor of Park Hill Methodist at the Howard Funeral Chapel, 17th Street and Marion, at 11 a.m. Friday morning, March 10. Members of the Eastern Star and Rainbow will participate in the final rites.

In addition to her son Stanley, other surviving members of Mrs. Goss' family are her mother Mrs. Beatrice Langford of Strasburg, a sister Mrs. Unave Bussell, 2373 Oakland, Aurora, a sister Mrs. Lillie Hammett, Yucca Valley, Calif, and a grandson, Christopher Goss.

Rocky Mountain News, Mar 10, 1961, p. 101.

Trying to Move on With a Life of Pain

I'd long learned to block out pain, clinging to my high adaptability to navigate life. I leaned into my work ethic and intellect and again pursued a good education, though not at the School of Mines. I then left Colorado and never looked back, effectively slamming the door on my past.

I moved to San Francisco, Los Angeles, and then Phoenix, eventually ending up in Houston, where I have lived for over thirty years. Tina and I were married for eleven years, long enough to have four kids: Chris, Heather, Steve, and Tim. I left the marriage, which caused lots of pain for everyone.

Yet, God is good. He provided me with a fantastic wife, Suzi, and her two kids, David and Lisa. We have been married for 48 years, and what splendid years they have been. We are in a great place today.

A few years ago, a lovely lady, Mary Bell, posed an interesting question to me, "How did you get this way?"

What a blessing of a question! How did I go from a talented young boy, deeply and profusely wounded by the deaths of my closest family members and leaving a massive heap of anguish and rubble behind, to arrive as such a man in such a prosperous place?

Yet, I knew the answer, and quickly: Only by God's grace. No other answer could attempt to make any sense at all. I couldn't begin to claim credit for the outcome of my journey. God has just brought me along for the ride. But the astonishing tales of His grace never end, and in my case, there is more to this story.

An Incredible Twist of Fate

About forty years after the deaths of my mom, Ruth, and sister, Nancy, probably in about 2003 or 2004, Suzi and I visited Galveston, Texas, about 1,200 miles from Denver. We enjoyed time together there with some friends, Gayle and Phil, at the art walk, and they brought along a couple that we didn't know, Skip and Susan Williams.

On the first night, we strolled around Galveston and stopped at a wine bar, enjoying glasses of wine and becoming acquainted with each other. At the time, Suzi and I owned a horse whom we discussed fondly. Susan remarked that she had once been involved with horses, but left equestrianism when she moved to Texas.

I asked her where she moved from. When she responded, "Colorado," that obviously piqued my interest. So, I inquired, "Where in Colorado?" and she answered, "Aurora."

What a coincidence! I thought.

"Where did you go to school?" I asked.

"Aurora Central."

We had attended the same school!

But then, the conversation turned bizarre. It so happened that Susan and I had lived a mere couple of blocks apart, but she was a few years younger, so we'd never known each other. As I turned away from the conversation, a bit befuddled, my wife picked it up and continued talking with Susan. Suzi told her that my mother and sister had been killed in an accident, and that I had moved back into the house after that.

Stunned, Susan grabbed Suzi's arm and asked, "Was his sister's name Nancy?"

Suzi, in turn, grabbed my arm.

Time stood still.

It turned out that Susan and Nancy had been good friends in junior high. Susan had clear memories of Nancy, my house, and even a brief memory of my mom. She recalled the accident clearly and had even been an honorary pallbearer.

She remembered me, although I don't recall the things she remembered. She described my funeral garb – a black suit – and said that I had handed roses to her and the other girls who served as honorary pallbearers.

The rest of that evening turned into a period of altered consciousness. The incredible "coincidence" of it all shocked me, and I think all of us. It reopened an old and very deep wound in me. The rest of our group was gentle, respectful, and more than a little awed. I will never forget that night. Although I can't remember much of the rest of the evening, I do remember feeling copiously touched, sad, and blessed.

How Ruth and Nancy's Deaths Saved a Family

The party and I shared breakfast together the next morning before my wife and I returned home to Houston. I had voiced that I believed this was God's way of offering me a reunion of sorts with my sister, Nancy. It did turn out that way, but more about that later.

When God's almighty hand shepherds, there is always more to a story. Following our experience in Galveston, we all parted ways. I later learned that in the aftermath, as Susan and Gayle discussed our meeting, Susan revealed more of her story. But, because of the emotional impact of our time in Galveston, Susan didn't want to unload the rest of her story on me that night. Yet, she yearned for me to know it, and asked Gayle share it with me.

Susan grew up, got married, had a son, got divorced, and then remarried. Her son, at age fifteen, did not get along well with her then-husband, a large man.

One night, her son knocked on their bedroom door and complained that he was feeling ill. The husband sent him back to his room, but the young man persisted, insisting that his symptoms were worsening.

After a while, Susan, by now also feeling sick, got up to check on her son. He appeared frighteningly sick, his face lifeless and pasty. At some point, Susan's theory shifted from "flu" to carbon monoxide gas poisoning. She grabbed him and they rushed outdoors onto the deck into a freezing cold night, and both soon felt a little better.

By then, her husband, whose larger body mass more slowly assimilated the gas, had begun to fall ill. When the family called for help, they soon discovered that the house was filled with gas due to a faulty furnace.

In a very real way, the deaths of my mother and fifteen-year-old sister years before end up saving the lives of Nancy's friend, Susan, her fifteen-year-old son, and her husband.

Upon hearing the rest of her story, I was rendered speechless, and my mind was riddled with questions. *What, if anything, was the meaning of these stunning events? Was it all just a random coincidence? Or was it more than that?*

A young boy experiences sudden, dramatic, and multiple tragic losses. He grows into a young man and meets further devastations. Yet, despite it all, he makes it down the crooked road of life and ends up in a very "good place."

Forty plus years and hundreds of miles later, he "randomly" meets a woman, with her own childhood experience of untimely loss of the same person, my sister, and her young friend. Could mere "arbitrary circumstances" possibly have brought these two people together? Why? Was there even an answer?

The gifts for me were twofold. One, the knowledge that, for Susan, the memory of Nancy's death saved the lives of herself and her family. Two, I benefited from getting to know my own sister better through the youthful memories of her friend.

A Reunion, of Sorts, with my Sister

After our encounter in Galveston, my wife and I saw Susan and Skip socially on occasion. We enjoyed each other's company, but the subject of Nancy never came up again. Our intertwined pasts forged a fundamental, but unspoken bond that needed a rest. After a few years passed, I realized I still had unfinished business.

I ached to write this story down and needed to finally have a conversation with Susan about her recollections of Nancy. I reached out to her, and she graciously agreed to meet for lunch and share what she could remember. As we began that luncheon conversation, Susan warned me that, at sixty-four years of age, she didn't remember a whole lot.

That meant Nancy, had she lived, would also have been sixty-four. I was seventy-one at the time, and that insight set a parameter which clarified some previous uncertainties.

As I calculated it in my mind, Nancy was seven years younger than me. I graduated from Aurora Central in 1956. Susan graduated in the Class of 1964, which meant Nancy would have graduated eight years after me. This was meaningful information and helped my mind finally fill in some blanks.

Susan first informed me that she noticed a "huge" family resemblance between Nancy and myself. I loved that! She recalled Nancy as perpetually smiling, wearing glasses, sporting jet-black hair, and striking, lightly colored eyes.

Just like me!

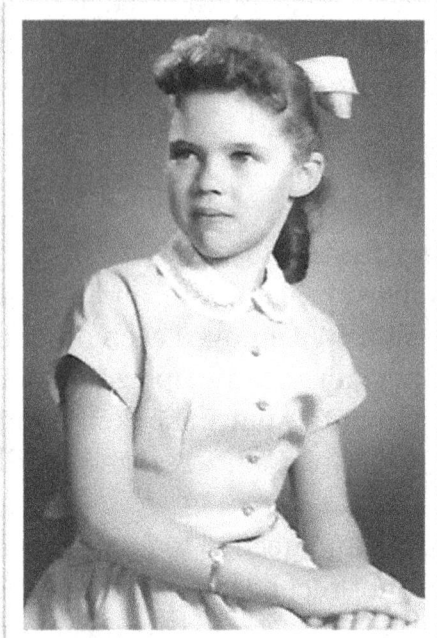 

According to Susan, Nancy possessed a bubbly, positive energy, and people were naturally attracted to her. The two met in junior high, in seventh or eighth grade. Susan, owning up to her past school-aged girl insecurities, viewed Nancy as a "real grown up."

"She wore sophisticated clothes, including lots of black," Susan recalled, which struck her as far more fashionable than the other girls. Susan regarded Nancy as more of a "leader person" and evidently considered my sister far more mature and bolder than her own siblings.

Nancy started a "girls club," which might be called a clique today. The sole club membership requirement was that all "members" wore tight black skirts and pink sweaters on a certain day of the week. Susan recalled fearing that her dad, a man tight with the dollar, wouldn't buy her the skirt and sweater. But her dad agreed, and she was delighted to be a part of Nancy's club.

The night we'd initially met in Galveston, Susan had mentioned how vividly she recalled my childhood house, in which Nancy, my mom, and I lived. In particular, she remembered the basement as a perfect hideout for parties. Susan and Nancy had held many "boy-girl" parties. Nothing bad happened there. The main reason most of the parties were hosted there was that my mom didn't interfere like other parents might.

It was in the domain of "boys" and "girls" that Susan and Nancy had a falling out. In Susan's words, "my infantile relationship with Nancy ended because of a lack of trust. As much as I was enamored with her, I think our friendship ended due to what I felt was a break in trust. I think she went after my boyfriend."

Susan recalled one last story about the darker side of Nancy's boldness and leadership. Unknown to any of the parents, the two girls occasionally took a bus to downtown Denver, which at that time was a very gutsy move for a couple of young teenage girls. On one return trip home, Nancy proudly displayed a new bracelet that she "mysteriously" acquired.

Nancy then took Susan back downtown to teach her how she "acquired" (shoplifted) the bracelet. Nancy then dared Susan to do the same. Susan could never muster up the guts to lift a bracelet but did eventually meet the "challenge" by taking a pair of sunglasses. She could never bring herself to wear it, and eventually gave it away. Hopefully, that was the end of the shoplifting, but we will never know.

The only other memory Susan could retrieve was of the funeral. She had been surprised to be invited to be an honorary pallbearer, since she and Nancy had fallen out. She then described me, a young man in that black suit, handing roses to the girls. It was a huge funeral for a mother and daughter, she said.

She depicted the funeral as a gray, gloomy day – an "out of body" experience for her. For me, it was an "out of mind" experience. The only image I kept was faint and fleeting: the funeral procession, which seemed to go on forever.

Strength and a Sense of Empowerment

Well, this is my origin story. I thought perhaps it deserved to be told and might possibly of interest to someone other than me. My sweet wife, Suzi, has assured me that, mostly, I needed to record it for myself.

As I have navigated through my adult life, I've observed other people's stories about their adult parents and siblings. I knew that I would have none of those stories to tell since, as an adult man, I have not had the opportunity to experience interacting with my own father or mother or a sibling. But God is good, and His grace has carried me through.

What I have experienced is tremendous healing over the tragic events that significantly impacted my childhood. My wounds have been transformed into gratitude and peace. My "reunion" with Nancy, thanks to Susan's generosity and heart, has given me a slightly deeper sense of who my sister was, and perhaps who she might have become.

At my age, I feel blessed to "know" her better now. Of course, there is no sure way to predict the uncertainties of life, but I believe that had Nancy and I lived to adulthood together, we would have become close friends. I do know, thanks to Susan's memory bank, that Nancy and I shared much in common. And, we would have had each other!

But things did not go that way, and God has instead led me along a different path. I am convinced that part of His kind plan of healing and redemption included bringing Susan into my path. And Susan has received her own gifts, as well.

After our lunch meeting, she said, "It was fun for me, today, to remember that time in my life. It was a big stretch for me to take the bus downtown with Nancy, for example, but it gave me courage to do other things later in high school. I would never have stopped putting a magnifying glass on this small space in my life. However, because of Nancy, I have. I'm seeing where the interaction with Nancy gave me strength and a sense of empowerment."

As for me, my journey continues. I have denied, ignored, confronted, raged, grieved, and celebrated the remnants of my past. The present for me is indeed blessed. The future looks bright. My faith has never been stronger. And my story is still being written.

When complete, I pray the artistic masterpieces comprised of those little slivers and big chunks of memory – molded out of my relationships and interactions with my family, friends, and anyone else whose path I have crossed – will, with God's grace, appear both beautiful to them and pleasing to Him.

Tears of Sorrow, Tears of Joy

Chapter 3

From Verbal to Written: How God's Grace Got the Words on the Page

For years, my rationale for not writing was that I was a "talker" not a writer.

The other narrative I repeatedly expressed to myself was that my stories were not significant in the overall scheme of the world. Yet that paradigm finally shifted for me after concluding the amazing story that you just read. For the first time in my life, I recorded my deepest pains, revelations, and growth on paper.

Along with encouragement from my beautiful wife, the denouement of the story motivated me to chronicle more tales. Foremostly, I felt God graciously steering me to write.

"Write about My grace in your life," I sensed the Lord saying to me. And, suddenly, stories began pouring out of me like a spring bursting forth, as they continue to do to this day. Many of these accounts are sprinkled throughout this book.

I remember a famous saying, "When an older person dies, a library burns down." My aim in the Crown of Glory Fellows Ministry, which I describe more in-depth in the pages ahead, is to encourage older women and men to write or record their journeys. Future generations can benefit, and there are people who will want to know.

I have shared some of my stories with my own ten beautiful grandkids who are each starting their own families, as well as others who have listened to (and sometimes even appeared to appreciate) them. I know that, without my uttering or typing them, once I am gone, no-one will know or remember who that Stan Goss guy was. It is my hope, and sole objective in recording my history, that people will say of me, "He was a man of God!"

Chapter 4
Demographic Realities of an Aging Population

At some point as I aged, perhaps in my 60s, my eyes began to open to the demographics of aging in our nation. People nowadays are living longer, as evidenced by the tidal wave of "Baby Boomers," or those born from the years 1946 to 1964. Baby Boomers still living are increasingly significant in the population, especially as they've begun exiting the workforce and entering a new stage of their lives: retirement.

For over a decade, the number of people retiring a day in the U.S. has been unprecedented: ten thousand people. This trend will continue into the 2030s.

The implications of this drift are enormous. The fastest growing age group in America, in percentage, is 100-year-olds. More people are living to reach 100 years of age than ever before in modern history. To place this in perspective, if you are fifty years old today, the Lord willing and if your health holds, you may have another fifty years of life ahead.

Yet, on the other end of the scale, birth rates in the U.S. and other "first world" countries have dropped below the levels capable of sustaining their countries and cultures.

The simple economic equation is as follows: In a capitalist society, when a baby is born, a future consumer is born. As that child grows into adulthood, he or she receives education, becomes a productive citizen, and eventually parents other impending consumers. The health and sustainability of a capitalist country depends on the continuation of this cycle.

Experts generally agree that the "magic number" for national viability is 2.2 children per family. When this number begins to drop, within two to three generations, sustainability wanes. Many Western European countries have documented birth rates well under 2.2 for a few decades.

For example, Italy, France, Germany, Spain, Greece, and Great Britain, along with other nations, have now declined to averages of 1.3 or less children born per family. In conjunction with fewer numbers of younger people paying into age-related entitlements dedicated to retirees, we are watching demonstrations in the streets for entitlements with no funding source. This is the same dilemma we face in America involving future funding of Social Security and Medicare.

The ramifications of this phenomenon extend even further. The declining numbers of younger people in the workforce along with an increasing number of elderly retirees poses a crucial question: Who will care for our world's elders in their end days?

Japan offers an acute example of this conundrum. Along with an alarmingly low 1.0 birthrate for decades, Japan has almost zero immigration. Japan, which has a culture of honoring elders, is experiencing the downfalls of this reality.

And then, there's America. Our nation continues to uphold the 2.2 figure. At face value, this appears sustainable, yet when this figure is dissected demographically and ethnically, a different story begins to emerge.

The birthrate among the American white population is at approximately 1.6; the black population is even less than that.

The declining black population is the consequence of decades of government policies that have discouraged the formation of black families and incentivized fatherless homes. These low family birth numbers are offset by Hispanic families, which average about 2.9 births per household. This factor, along with a massive wave of immigration from the south of the U.S. border, will dictate the future trends of our population.

The moral of this story is as follows; ¡Es muy importante hablar Español, amigos!

You may wonder about the primary determinants in family size. The fundamental familial "birth control," or family size reduction influencer, is wealth. Statistics reveal that the richer the family, the less children they tend to have. This is a direct outcome of the last several decades of prosperity in our nation. Our nation's middle class has enjoyed the majority of this prosperity, yet have birthed fewer children, and the average family size has diminished.

On the other hand, a principal factor that contributes to large families is religion. Religious families tend to have more children. This accounts for the high birth rate of Latino families, who are chiefly religious and Roman-Catholic. This trend is similar among most Christian denominations in America, although ongoing cultural attacks on the church and its people are beginning to shift the waters.

Examine today's Western Europe and its rapidly morphing sociocultural atmosphere. In England, the familial birth average has averaged under 1.3 births per family for the past few decades. The nation's Christian population has diminished dramatically, alongside an ongoing flood of entering refugees from Muslim countries. The average Islamic family births approximately 9 kids per family. Just do the math!

Furthermore, the U.S. has its own troubling math to consider. As the Baby Boomers, ten thousand per day, leave work and enter retirement, the entitlements for this generation increase exponentially. As you recall, their numbers, and thus, entitlements, are growing aggressively. Meanwhile, the shrinking population of younger workers are responsible for footing this bill.

These events, compounded by botched and irresponsible governmental policies, are brewing a catastrophic storm. Our annual federal deficit since 2002 has transitioned from below zero (the U.S. had budget surpluses in 1998-2001) to trillions of dollars today. As I write this, our current deficit, along with unfunded entitlements, amounts to $155,423,034,729,000 ($155 trillion). And since I've written this chapter, this number has continued to hike at a terrifying rate.

Our nation's current deficit can be broken down to $986,000 owed per taxpayer. This is just shy of a million dollars. To place these numbers in perspective:

> 1 Million seconds equals 12 days
> 1 Billion seconds equals 32 years
> 1 Trillion seconds equals 32,320 years

For my math enthusiasts, multiply 32,200 by 155 to begin to grasp the unprecedented national bankruptcy that has already been created.

Where God Took Me on This Issue

"Retirement is not a biblical concept!" As I speak on this topic, I aim to encourage, inspire, and motivate that growing segment of the population – the aging and elderly – to "stay in the game of life."

I urge this group, blessed with the gift of aging, to remain or become involved and healthy. In my speaking, I draw a lot on a great book entitled *Younger Next Year: A Guide to Living Like 50 Until You're 80 and Beyond* by Chris Crowley and

Henry Lodge, M.D. (Workman Publishing Company, 2005; 2007; 2019). This book is a great resource, stockpiled with tips and ideas about aging "younger." I highly recommend it. Here are some of the cornerstone concepts:

- Aging is natural, decay is optional. Seventy percent of premature death and aging is lifestyle related. Much of this can be offset through exercise, which is your master signal for growth to your body. Thus, you must exercise six days a week for the rest of your life and engage in serious weight training twice a week: period.

- It's up to you to decide between retirement and decay, or growth and healthy aging. Life is but an endurance event, which must be trained for, long and slow.

A few more suggestions include the following:

- Whiten your teeth.
- Drink more water.
- Spend less than you make.
- Your diet should be basic: don't eat crap and avoid fad diets.
- Lay off sugar.
- Drink in moderation. In fact, do all things in moderation.
- Care, connect and commit with people.
- Tell your stories.
- Smile and laugh a lot.
- Create a pack.
- Never, ever retire from life.
- Say yes to everything. Make "yes" your favorite answer.

I've added a couple more bullets of my own:

- Be a geek, not a geezer.
- As you age, don't let your fear of technology keep you out of the game.
- Additionally, be bolder as you get older. This I will expand upon later.

Chapter 5
I've had 62 Jobs, but I'd Always Wanted to be a Coach

Farm kids work. From the beginning of my young life on the farm, at age six or seven, I was responsible for laborious chores. Milking cows, feeding chickens and pigs, churning butter, and ice cream; work was what I did.

I acquired my first paying job when I was a baby-faced six-year-old. I herded our neighbor's cows for a dollar a day. I would sit on my horse, my saddlebags stocked full of comic books and peanut butter and jelly sandwiches, and I'd shepherd cow after cow, all day.

Then, the men in my family all passed away. My mother packed our bags and moved us into the city of Aurora, a suburb of Denver, where I spent my teenage years. I always had multiple jobs: sacking groceries, heading a newspaper route, mowing lawns, and carrying hod for bricklayers. With a sturdy farm boy's work ethic, I was a firm proponent of earning my own spending money.

When I reached my college years, I maintained multiple part-time jobs: working in the mailroom of a hospital, serving as a management analyst for the Colorado State Government, working the graveyard shift at the Greyhound racing track in the money room, and making boxes at the Coors brewery in Golden, Colorado.

These don't begin to scratch the varying jobs I've worked. I could probably write a separate book about all the occupations I've held, but I'll just list some highlights.

AT&T Long Lines Division
- Denver, Human Resources
- Denver, Plant Manager
- San Francisco, Military Network Project Installation Manager
- San Francisco, Engineering Project Program Coordinator
- Los Angeles, Major Interstate Accounts Sales Manager

Union Bank
- Los Angeles, Business Development Officer

United Bank
- Phoenix, Business Development Officer

Lazarus and Sanders (Public Accounting Firm)
- Principal, Client Relations, and Client Management

Kelso Earth Shoe Store
- Phoenix and Mesa, Arizona, Franchise Owner

American Teller Schools
- Houston, Texas, Owner

Goss and Associates (Executive Search Firm specializing in Banking and Corporate Finance)
- Houston, Texas, Owner

King, Chapman, and Broussard (Senior Executive Outplacement Firm)
- Houston, Texas, Managing Director

The Mastery Group (Senior Executive Leadership Coaching Firm)
- Houston, Texas, Managing Director

Out of all my work, managing my coaching firm has been the highlight of my professional career.

Tears of Sorrow, Tears of Joy

Chapter 6

How a Talented but Difficult Executive Helped Me Launch My Executive Coaching Career

Outplacement is defined as a service paid for by a company to a professional firm to support the career or life transition of an employee released or terminated by the employer. The Outplacement Firm provides the separated individual with counseling or coaching, assessment tools, clerical support, and sometimes office space.

Joining the Senior Executive Outplacement Firm was the perfect move for me. I had previously, through our Executive Search Firm, placed several thousand corporate executives.

I was familiar with all the employment processes and had an extensive network of old friends, clients, and relationships to call upon. This relationship building continued to help ease more people through their career transitions.

One day, I got a call from one of our client companies; they were preparing for another termination. The individual they aimed to let go was a "talented but difficult" executive who brought great value to the company, but exhibited some behaviors that were detrimental to their overall performance.

So, they have a talented, yet difficult, executive. The relationship seemed salvageable to me, so I asked the company if they would like to keep the individual employed. To this, they responded, "Yes, but no-one has been able to get this man to change, and we aren't optimistic that he ever will."

Unflustered, I suggested that they let me work with him. They agreed.

Thus began an intervention, rather than an outplacement. The corporate realm was different back then. We didn't even know what to call our approach, so we coined it "executive coaching." In those days, executive coaching was a very new idea, and its specifics were relatively unknown.

In this man's case, I am delighted to say, he was highly coachable and sufficiently motivated to make the difficult changes necessary to keep his job. His situation served as a win-win for all parties involved: the company, the man, his employees and co-workers, and his family.

I have future plans to write another, in-depth book about my thirty-year coaching practice, called "The Mastery Group," but right now, I will leave you with a few fundamental lessons I've learned.

1) People can change, if they have a good enough reason to do so.

2) It is better to invest your coaching money in the best "athletes," be it CEOs, tech workers, designers and so on. These high performers tend to be the most coachable.

3) If a person proves un-coachable (coachability defined as possessing an openness to look at themselves and change), they will unilaterally become a waste of everyone's time, energy, and money.

As I further delved into my coaching career, I became an avid student of leadership and human behavior. These two mechanisms merged into the fundamental purpose of my work: leadership development.

As my client successes grew, my practice grew. People experienced the tremendous value of our work together, and they wanted more. My network of contacts and referrals sprouted exponentially.

One morning, I rose out of bed at the middle age of fifty-two. I had held sixty-two jobs and was now known as "Coach." In fact, to this day, many people still lovingly refer to me as "Coach." When I'm asked about this nickname, I smile and respond, "I have always wanted to be a coach. As a once young athlete, I had no father or grandfather, but my athletic coaches looked after me, nurtured me, and encouraged me."

Yet when it came time to make a college decision, I was advised not to go into coaching because it was a low-paying profession with a high turnover rate.

I was a sharp kid, so my advisors urged me to select a career that paid well. I was fortunate to have good choices. I was offered an appointment with the US Naval Academy and a full scholarship with the Colorado School of Mines, the premiere academic university in the fields of petroleum and earth sciences.

Yet, life is ironic. Thirty-plus years later, and many jobs later, there I was, coaching, and making good money to boot.

My blessings were divine. An increasingly lucrative career in coaching spanned my next thirty years on this earth. What follows is a partial client list:

The University of Texas Medical Center
I spent ten years working with the president, Dr. John Stobo, and his senior leadership team. Many thanks to Dr. Kathy Shingleton for bringing me there.

JP Morgan Chase Bank, Texas and New York
Over the years, I coached dozens of senior executives.

Marc Ecko
In the course of four years, I conducted extensive work with the senior leaders of this $1 billion dollar retail clothing manufacturer.

ABC Nightline, Washington, D.C.
I worked with Ted Koppel and his team to affect a major organizational transition. Thanks to Tom Bettag for bringing me there.

NACE (National Association of Corrosion Engineers)
I proudly facilitated seven years of collaborative success in leadership development work with this global association of 35,000 members, including creating multiple leadership academies. Thanks to their leader, Bob Chalker, for bringing me there and sharing the glory of the work.

Houston Texans, Professional football team
Thanks to my dear friend, Bubba Levy, for bringing me there.

Houston Symphony
With the symphony, I embarked on a year of major transformational processes to bring the symphony back from the brink of total failure. Thanks again to Bubba Levy for bringing me there.

Greater Houston Partnership
I spent seven years coaching with the brilliant leader Jeff Moseley and his senior leader team. Thanks to Chairman Jodie Jiles for bringing me there.

PPL, Allentown, PA
I worked throughout the region with this major interstate power provider, including in collaboration with the leadership team at Three Mile Island Nuclear Plant. Thanks to Ron Schwarz for bringing me there for a wonderful two years.

PSEG, Newark, NJ
I enjoyed over two years of leadership development and coaching work with this NJ and PA major regional power provider. Thanks to Ron Schwarz for bringing me there.

Alvarez and Marsal, New York and Houston
I engaged in team coaching and leadership development. Thanks to Jeff Smith and Tom Elsenbrook for bringing me there.

Burlington Resources, ConocoPhillips, and Rosetta Resources
I worked with the brilliant leader Randy Limbacher and his senior teams. Thanks to Randy for bringing me along.

Global Pipe and Supply
I worked closely with President Art Shelton and his senior team. Thanks to Art for letting me share his leadership genius.

Others included:
- MD Anderson Cancer Center
- Baylor College of Medicine
- Global Pipe and Supply
- Houston Methodist Hospital
- Texas Children's Hospital

Clients

The Mastery Group is proud to be affiliated with the following clients

Partial Client List

J.P. Morgan Chase Bank
M. D. Anderson Cancer Center
Texas Children's Hospital
American Tower
Time Warner Cable
ABC Nightline
American General Insurance
University of Texas Medical Branch
Tubescope Vetco
Alvarez and Marsal
Echo Unlimited
Deloitte Touche
Houston Texans Football Team
Houston Symphony
PPL
3DI
Rosetta Resources
Varco International
St. Luke's Hospital
PSEG
Sterling Bank
ConocoPhillips

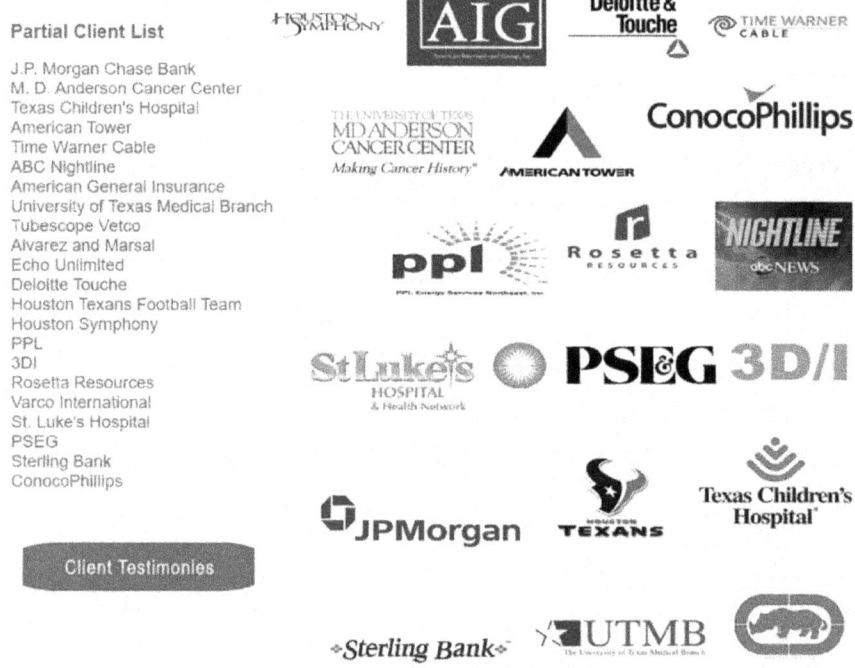

Client Testimonies

Katy-Area Economic Development Council

I was also blessed to serve on the Board of Governors for this incredible organization, where I led the Leadership Committee for over fifteen years. I coached our great leader, Lance LaCour, and his staff, including the impressive Angie Thomason and Vanessa Wheeless. I also served our brilliant Board Chairman, Paul Kurt, and our Chairman and Leader of almost twenty years, Woody Mann.

Great things are happening at the Katy Area EDC. In fact, I am still there as an Emeritus Board member. Major thanks to the beloved Stan Stanley for bringing me here.

Once more, God continues to connect the tiny, seemingly endless dots that comprise my life. As you read forward and learn more about the Crown of Glory Fellows Ministry, you will clearly see how all the tools I've developed from my coaching career are now in play to serve the Lord and his people.

Tears of Sorrow, Tears of Joy

Chapter 7
Growing Clarity and Awareness of "The Answers Within"

As an integral aspect of my highly successful thirty-year executive leadership coaching practice, I developed many models as coaching tools. My models were catered toward areas like change, relationships, being an integral person and more.

For several years now, I have been teaching others those models. As I have stepped into the role of teacher, the Holy Spirit has continually shown me how each model is simple, but profound, biblical wisdom.

Over the years, whenever I initiated a new client relationship, I told the client that the basis for our work together was this: their answers were already within them. Together, we would create processes and open dialogue to pull those answers out into the physical realm. We would relish in these "Aha!" moments and epiphanies.

Now, I finally understand that these "answers within" come from an absolute awakening to the fruits and the gifts of the Holy Spirit within. It took a mere eighty-two years to bring this full truth to light!

Tears of Sorrow, Tears of Joy

Chapter 8

From Focus on the World to Focus on the Word

I had entered my 70s, a golden decade in my life. These were my most prosperous and productive years. I was flourishing in my professional executive coaching practice and blessed with a large and loyal group of clients who were paying me extremely well. Our relationships were symbiotic. They felt they were receiving great value from our work together. Life was easy and good.

Then, God showed up once more to steer my path. The senior pastor of our church at the time was a man who massively influenced my life, Jim Leggett. Rooted in a passion to preach and teach through all sixty-six books of the Bible, our church founded a comprehensive, strategic Bible study program. The success of that program eventually led to the formation of The Bible Seminary as an independent, non-denominational 501(c)3 institution of higher education.

At the graying age of seventy-one, I enrolled in the original eight-semester certificate course of study. And at some point along the way, the demographic conversation I'd been contemplating crossed paths with the Word.

While reflecting one day, I experienced an epiphany. *I had the privilege of inspiring the older generation!* Palming my Bible, I flipped through the pages and found its index, and there it was:

> "Gray hair is a crown of glory; it is gained in a righteous life." (Proverbs 16:31)

This Scripture hit me with a monumental magnitude, and behold, I embarked on the next leg of my journey. The Crown of Glory Fellows Ministry was born.

My purpose – which initially was to inspire, encourage, and activate the elder generations – expanded. Now, I have become driven to inspire elders to serve as kingdom builders in their final years.

My body, mind, and soul were ablaze. I was invigorated by the Lord's new purpose for me, and intrigued with the unknown paths to which this might lead.

Chapter 9
On the Invisibility of Aging

I founded my bread and butter, an executive leadership coaching practice, at age fifty-two.

After numerous trials and tribulations, my practice grew and flourished. In my work, I utilized multiple industry-leading assessment tools to benefit my clients. These tools gauged factors such as "Strengths and Weaknesses" and "Preferred Styles of Leadership" along many other metrics.

The best tool at my disposal was the "Birkman Method." The creator of this wonderful tool, Dr. Roger Birkman, was a fresh-faced alum from the University of Houston with a doctorate in Psychology during World War II. Fascinated with stress and the causes of stress, the doctor developed a scientifically valid tool to evaluate this phenomenon.

I once believed that the most important questions you can ask yourself in life are "What is it about me? Why do I do the things I do that work so well? Why do I do things, sometimes, that don't work so well? Why do I get along with this person, and not that person?"

These questions encompass self-awareness. As I've grown in life, my primary question is now, "What is it about God and me?" But my second question remains, "What is it about me?"

The Birkman Method is essentially a way to understand yourself and your unique complexities. As a coach, I'm fond of it because it helps me understand you. What makes you tick? What causes you to do well? What are your growth opportunities?

For you, it's a tool for self-awareness and a great relational tool between two people. I often speak about relationships. All relationships begin with romance. We're encapsulated with each other, or perhaps someone is looking for a good job and another party is seeking a good employee. So, we get together, start living together, and then, disappointment sets in.

Disappointment overshadows relationships when we don't anticipate stressors in advance. The Birkman Method is also an excellent tool to predict those stressors, shortcomings, and potential clashes of ourselves and between us and our loved ones, employers, or employees.

It's also a phenomenal tool in team building, as leaders ask, "How do we optimize our positions?" and so on.

Over time, the Birkman Method has become what I've dubbed the "Gold Standard of Assessment Tools." Millions of profiles have been created to access his metric test, spanning the globe and many languages. In my career, with this tool at my disposal, I have interpreted thousands of profiles.

In his later years, even following the loss of his precious wife, Sue, Roger continued his work. His work ethic was tremendous. In the mornings, he would wake up and fetch a ride to The Houstonian Club, where he'd complete his daily work out. Then, he would suit up and head to the office.

And by coincidence, or more likely by God's shepherding hands, I just so happened to be present one morning when Roger walked into work.

The doctor wore a suit and tie, but by then, his clothing pooled at the edges, appearing a bit too large. I have since come to realize that as we grow older, we can grow smaller. I once stood a solid five-feet and eleven-inches tall. I am now five-feet-seven-inches and have become a frequenter at the tailor's as I've shortened the pants length on each of my suits.

At the time of our meeting, Dr. Birkman was ninety-two, and I was a mere seventy-two. I introduced myself, declaring him a role model. I confided in him my hopes that the next two decades of my life would be as fruitful as his.

The doctor was polite and expressed appreciation, but he professed, "The older we get, the more invisible we become."

I was stunned. Before me was a master, so brimming with knowledge and wisdom. He was a man who had contributed so much to so many. My conceptions had led me to believe legions would clamor to come and sit at his feet.

As you read on, I will crystallize how this reality has energized and motivated the Crown of Glory Fellows Ministry. Over a decade has passed since I met the doctor, and almost one year since his passing. During the span of those years I, too, have begun to experience this distinct phenomenon: the invisibility of aging.

So, I was out in the world, a fire boring through my belly, searching for places to bring my vision for this ministry into fruition. I visited the executive pastor of my church, who kindly listened to my story, and then responded, "I'm sorry Stan, but there is nothing we can do for you here."

That experience certainly wounded me, but I undauntedly kept advancing down the crooked path of life. I eventually stumbled upon a large group of gray-haired men who shared my passion. We brainstormed together, organized a one-day event, commenced inviting folks, and printed mountains of flyers to announce the event.

I then ventured back to my own church and approached our senior pastor. Equipped with the knowledge that the pastor met monthly with about thirty local pastors, I asked if he would take some flyers to distribute to their group.

"No!"

He abruptly dismissed me, informing me that their group shared a mutual "covenant" not to promote "events." Needless to say, his response crushed me.

In fairness, a few years later, we discussed the episode. He expressed remorse, and we prayed about it together. Perhaps something positive can come of it, but I leave that up to God, since I am on His clock. I simply press on, one day at a time.

I continued to print flocks of Crown of Glory business cards and frequently stuffed them in the palms of willing takers. I am currently on my third box of five-hundred cards. And I visit frequently with a group of older men who attend another church in my area. These men meet every Thursday morning at a local Whataburger.

I was at that fast food restaurant one morning when their senior pastor walked in and sat across from me. To provide some context, I had recently read an article titled *Ageism in the Church*. The premise of the article was about the massive enthusiasm in many churches to attract and recruit youth. The elders, by and large, are simply ignored. Sound familiar?

While emphasizing this issue to the pastor, he turned to me and said, "There is a reason for that, you know. We already have you guys." And I couldn't refute this! It was true then, and it is true now.

So why is the Crown of Glory Fellows Ministry so vital to the future of the church? I will explain more as my story progresses and the concept of elderly invisibility resurfaces in what I have titled the "Hidden in Plain Sight Army of Spiritual Warriors."

Chapter 10
Along Comes Colson

I have come to see that every person God puts before me presents the possibility of a divine intervention.

One of those impossibly impactful people, one of so many for me, was and is Kip Thompson. Kip was a familiar face from our church and a man whom I had met a few times. One day, he reached out to me to share a ministry that echoed in his head and heart: the Colson Fellows Program.

Chuck Colson was a prominent figure sentenced to prison as a result of the Nixon "Watergate" scandal. While behind bars, Colson came to Christ and founded Prison Fellowship International to minister to inmates. Colson became alarmed by the emerging culture war that was, and still is, being waged across our country.

Perhaps you're familiar with this battle already: the clash between Biblical Worldview and the Progressive Multicultural Worldview.

To reach the broader population, Colson created a Colson Fellows program designed to equip and inspire people to articulate and defend the Biblical Worldview. This knowledge is essential today, especially given the brigade of unique and unprecedented issues confronting our society and culture.

Colson Fellows generally meet mid-summer through late spring in local and regional groups around the world. The program calls for a major commitment of time, attention, and learning. Intrigued, I joined a cohort in my community that included fourteen people. We met at The Bible Seminary one Saturday a month for ten months.

Our modest cohort read around twenty books, listened to content expert speakers, participated in speaking projects, and worked as teams. Our goal was for each member to leave with what we referred to as a "ministry plan." Some struggled with that. I knew, both entering and leaving, that my calling was the Crown of Glory Fellows Ministry.

I was eighty years old when I completed the program and became a Colson fellow.

To this day, I continue to record my stories as a part of my personal ministry.

Chapter 11
Finishing Well with Grace

Life is a Marathon

The Oxford Dictionary defines coincidence as "a remarkable concurrence of events or circumstances without apparent causal connection."

Grace is "the free and unmerited favor of God as manifested in the salvation of sinners, through Christ, and the bestowal of blessings."

Jim Leggett

My wife, Suzi, and I were in between churches. We had scoured the area and visited a few different places, but so far, had not found a church that seemed a clear fit. We sought a "Holy Spirit prompting" to beckon to us. Our worlds changed when Suzi's good friend, Patti, invited us to visit her church.

Patti, and her husband, Rick, attended Grace Fellowship United Methodist Church in Katy, Texas. At the time, it was a relatively new and rapidly growing worship center in our area. It met on grounds that had once been part of The Great Southwest Equestrian Center and was a multi-acre, multi-facility campus.

I will never forget the morning we stepped foot into the church. The worship team, led by A.J. Bass, was performing lively music that flowed through the church grounds and energized the service. It was very different from the traditional hymns Suzi and I experienced growing up.

We learned that the music was called "contemporary." A.J., whom my daughter later referred to as "Hootie" because of his close resemblance to Darren Rucker (known as "Hootie" in the group Hootie and the Blowfish) moved the congregation to their feet, many with palms facing upward and worshipping with vigor and joy.

It was in that moment I felt the voice of God beckoning, "Welcome Home!"

But the best aspect unfolded after the praise and worship ended. It took shape in the form of the young pastor who founded the church a couple of years earlier: Jim Leggett.

Jim is a Texas A&M Aggie through and through. A proud engineering major, he refers to himself as an "engineering nerd." But what is most fundamental about Jim is that he has been and continues to be a devoted and profound teacher of the Bible, the Holy Word of God. I have been a church-going Christian all my life, but Jim Leggett has taught me more about the Bible than any other man.

In later years, Jim was inspirational in the creation of The Bible Seminary, which offers in-depth, comprehensive, strategic studies of the entire Bible from Genesis to Revelation. In addition to seminars, certificate, and degree studies, the seminary offers educational exhibits, study tours, productions, and publications. I received my eight-semester "Bible Certificate" from TBS at the age of seventy-five.

I could speak sermons about Jim Leggett, but for the purpose of this story, I will provide anecdotes illustrating what Jim has meant to me in my Faith Walk.

Waldo Leggett

Jim's father, Waldo, was highly involved in the Grace Fellowship church and held many leadership roles. I never knew Waldo closely, and to this day, I only recall a couple of brief conversations with him.

Yet, I was familiar with Waldo in a different way. He and I shared a riveting common ground – we were both serious runners and endurance athletes who regularly participated in many running events around the area. Waldo was a couple of years older than me, so most of the time, we competed in separate age groups, running distances which ranged from 10K to full 26.1-mile marathons.

In my mid-fifties, I took up cycling. I was enamored with the sport. The camaraderie of training and riding in events enthralled me. I participated in the MS 150 from Houston to Austin. I cycled in the "Hotter'N Hell Hundred" in Wichita Falls, Texas, an event held in the heat of summer that drew fifteen thousand cyclists every year. In many events, I enjoyed the privilege of cycling with several family members.

Some of my fondest memories from this period of my life were riding a two-seater tandem with my son, Steve, from Houston to Austin over the hills around Bastrop. My wife and my daughter-in-law, Jackie, rode the same tandem in Wichita Falls. My youngest son, Dave, once missed a turn and rode fifty miles instead of his planned twenty-five!

Obviously, I was very fit in those days. Enthused, I set a goal to participate in the Iron Man Triathlon in Hawaii by the age of fifty-five. This annual event kicks off with a two-mile swim in the ocean, followed by a 112-mile bike ride around the island of Oahu, and finishes with a 26.2-mile marathon run. This triathlon is an incredible test of fitness, discipline, and fierceness of will-to-win over pain.

Sadly, I never accomplished this goal. Although I profited from natural gifts as a runner and cyclist, my swimming was abysmal. Try as I did, I never overcame my lifetime of fear of the water. After a few months of floundering attempts at swimming training, I abandoned my triathlon aspirations.

Around the same time, I suffered from difficult injuries, primarily battle scars earned from running and cycling. I traded in my running shoes for golfing shoes and shifted my focus toward golf, a game I continue to deeply enjoy.

But Waldo Leggett carried on. He was a great competitor in the Seniors' Circuit throughout all three triathlon sports and won the 2011 World Triathlon Championship in his age group at age 76 in Beijing. Remarkably, as far as I know, Waldo continued to swim right up to the very end of his life.

A few years back, Suzi and I were digging through boxes of memorabilia when we stumbled across a small, yellowed clipping. The aging paper was an excerpt from the *Houston Chronicle*, listing the times of Houston runners who had competed in the 1984 Boston Marathon. This elite event required runners to run a qualifying time in a preliminary marathon. I had qualified with a previous Boston Marathon completion time of three hours and fourteen minutes (3:14). It wasn't my best. My personal best was 2:46:46, which had won me the U.S. Championship for my age group.

YEAR	GENDER	TIME	FIRST	LAST	RESIDENCE
1984	M	3:15:36	Stanley B	Goss	Texas
1984	M	3:26:44	L Waldo Jr	Leggett	Texas

As I scanned the 1984 Boston Marathon list, I noticed something amazing. Right behind my name was Waldo Leggett, who had run a 3:26, an excellent time for his age group. I hadn't realized that Waldo and I had both run Boston that year. I shared this with his son, Pastor Jim, and we shared a chuckle over it. I never spoke about it with Waldo, whom I believe was experiencing some health issues at that time

Waldo passed away on September 1, 2019. Jim bore a beautiful tribute to the godly man his father was. Like me, Waldo was born in Midland, Texas. He was a man of many marvelous athletic achievements:

- Twelve marathons, including New York and Boston
- Thirty triathlons
- World Triathlon Champion and U.S. representative for his age group in Beijing (2011)

I was struck by the vivid image Jim painted of his father's transition from this world to the next. He battled through pain, ventured through a dark tunnel, and emerged into an unimaginable stadium full of light, angelic celebration, joy, peace, and glory forever. This is heaven. He was and is in the company of Jesus, almighty God, angels, and all of the loved ones who had arrived before him. Astonishing and beautiful!

Hebrews 12:1-2 exhorts, "Therefore, since we are surrounded by so great a cloud of witnesses, let us also lay aside every weight, and sin which clings so closely, and let us run with endurance the race that is set out before us, looking to Jesus, the founder of our faith, who for the joy that was set before Him endured the cross, despising the shame, and is seated at the right hand of the throne of God."

I'm again compelled to explore why I am sharing these fragments of my life. I first recorded this story when I was eighty-one. I am now eighty-four. I have remained fascinated by the possible meanings this could convey.

Waldo Leggett, Sr.

A few years ago, we were once again rummaging through boxes of memorabilia, and I came across my birth certificate. It was a weathered piece of paper that recorded the details of my entrance into this life. I was born on September 18, 1938 in Midland, Texas. I don't remember other specifics, such as weight and length, but I'm sure I was a bouncing baby boy.

But as my eyes pulled further down the page, I was startled to see the signature of the attending physician, the doctor who delivered me into earth: "L. Waldo Leggett." I was stunned. Could there possibly be two Waldo Leggetts?

I immediately reached out to Pastor Jim. He revealed to me that L. Waldo was his grandfather, the father of Waldo. In the late 1930s, Dr. Leggett was the only doctor in the very small Texas town of Midland, which hosted a population of four thousand or so at that time. He attended to most of the medical needs of the community, including delivering babies.

Jim and I were both astonished at this remarkable coincidence. I raved to him how wonderful it was to know that his grandfather had brought me into this world, and Jim was helping me get out of it!

There is an African proverb that reads, "When an old man (or woman) dies, a library burns to the ground." I yearn to be remembered as a godly man; a man who lived a pretty interesting, grace-filled life. I have so many stories to tell about my blessing of a time here. And, by the way, so do you!

One of my favorite books is *How to Finish the Christian Life; Following Jesus in the Second Half*, by Donald W. Sweeting and George Sweeting (Moody Publishers 2012). In the last chapter, "Give 'em Heaven!" the authors describe the Christian life as a long-distance journey that requires a marathon mindset. They end with "two final things to say."

First, you are not dead yet. You have time, still, to forge the story of your life and build a legacy. Who knows how long you have? Is it one year? Is it five? Is it twenty; forty? You do not know how many days God has numbered for you. Let this notion energize you. As long as you have today, make it count.

Second, as you encounter the people and culture around you, "give 'em heaven!" As we bless others in the name of Christ, may they catch a glimpse of a better land and a more lasting kingdom. By the grace of God and the Spirit's power, may they be wooed through our lives and our corporate witness into joining us on the journey. Yes, yes, yes...give 'em heaven!

I have come to see that the ultimate manifestation of God's grace is Heaven itself.

He created us, gave us life, gave us dominion, gave us free will, and when we failed, He gave us Himself as Jesus. He welcomes us home with open arms, after our crooked and unique journeys through a strange and interesting land.

The spirit of Jesus in me greets the spirit of Jesus in you. May this bring us together toward the Father and the Son and the Holy Spirit!

Amen!

Chapter 12

Men's Work and God's Perfect Plan

"If you build it, they will come."

At the beginning of this book, you read the astonishing story of tragedies in my life that led to grace. There is more to that story.

After a traumatic personal loss that rendered me almost alone in the world, I was a young, unprepared father, deeply wounded, yet still a golden child. I spent the next thirty-two years wandering around, trying to make my mark. I had multiple jobs and business ventures which were neither great successes nor great failures.

Someone once asked me what stood out as a turning point for me. I answered, "Field of Dreams."

Field of Dreams

One night Suzi and I went out with our dear friends, Pam and Bill, to see a new baseball movie starring Kevin Costner. *Field of Dreams* (1989) is a profoundly metaphysical story that incorporates three cryptic messages: 1) "If you build it, he will come," 2) "Ease his pain," and 3) "Go the distance."

In it, Costner's character, Ray Kinsella, builds a baseball field in the middle of a cornfield on his rural Iowa farm that ends up hosting ghosts of late baseball players.

Ray loses his father at an early age, which inflicts deep wounds in his core. When the ghost, or spirit, of his young dad arrives, the two end up playing catch together by the corn.

That scene triggered something profound within me. At the age of fifty-two, a memory resurfaced of myself as a young boy standing on my family farm and playing catch with my own dad by the corn, beside the very field where he died.

Tears began flowing from my eyes and didn't dry for a month or so. The depths of my pain, which I had cloaked for so long by maintaining my composure and "looking good," was now fully exposed. I had cried all my life, even though I had been chastised by my sports coaches that "men don't cry."

Now, I understand why I cried. I have solely one vague memory as that young boy of crying at all the funerals of dear ones that I had lost.

Weekend Warrior

Shortly after this experience, a friend named Al Levy asked me to lunch. He wanted to share a weekend event he had just experienced in Wisconsin. He then asked me about my story, and as I shared the emotions I was experiencing, he nodded widely and said, "This weekend is for you."

I drove straight from lunch back into the office, called the weekend coordinator and registered to go to Wisconsin for one of the upcoming events. The cost was six hundred dollars, plus roundtrip airfare. At the time, my wife and I were really struggling financially, and this expense was heavy.

So, I phoned my wonderful wife and told her that I was going and what it cost. She asked me what it was all about. I told her I had no idea why, but that I felt called to go. She said, "Then go." That's the kind of incredible wife God gave me.

I realize now that this was the beautiful prompting of the Holy Spirit. Attending that weekend changed my life forever. The weekend was transformative and healing. Its impact on me continued throughout the next twenty or so years of my life, and I poured myself into this "work."

Eventually, my four sons completed the weekend in Wisconsin. I became a leader, and played a big role, along with many other "brothers," in bringing the weekends to Texas.

Our Texas and Louisiana community grew into several thousand men. One of the men donated land near Madisonville, Texas, and the community built a retreat center there called "Land of My Grandfathers." That site is still utilized by many different groups of both men and women.

I became a weekend leader and personally led over a hundred weekends. I also trained and developed many men into becoming leaders. This was the genesis of my thirty-year executive leadership coaching practice.

One critical part of the process was to wake men up by teaching them to understand their emotional nature. I became somewhat of an expert on a subject which became has known as emotional intelligence, or "EQ" (emotional quotient).

But the nature of all things is to change. Originally called "The New Warrior Adventure Weekend," the organization changed its name to "The Mankind Project" and soon took a hard left turn into progressive multiculturalism.

During this time, a growing group of conservative Christian "New Warriors" became exasperated with the new dogma of progressivism. One event served as a tipping point and inspired the group to organize a "Christ-centered New Warrior Weekend."

This budding, new event was a weekend experience which included all the foundational processes of the "New Warrior Training Adventure," but also included prayer, a cross, and Scripture.

The weekend was billed as such, and some men opted out, but many others were inspired to join. The effect of the weekend on all participants was profound. But following the weekend, the "progressives" threw a hissy fit over its occurrence, even though they were not present to experience it for themselves. Tragically, their ideology blocked their own ability to see reality.

It became clear that it was time for me to move on. I was well-known and respected as one of the founders of the experience. Yet, as an older, white, Christian, conservative man, to the new leadership – unless I was willing to recant all I stood for – I was *persona non-grata*. I realized that God had stationed me there for a season and for a purpose. I fulfilled my purpose, and then I left.

I have nothing but gratitude for my time as a New Warrior. The healing, joy, learning, transformation, and life-long relationships that resulted from my twenty-five years there helped shape my life. I would not be the man I am today without it.

Tears of Sorrow, Tears of Joy

Chapter 13
My Father's Ring, My Father's Blessing, and Tears of Joy

One of the key elements of the New Warrior experience was that after men completed their initial weekend, they stratified into small groups of eight to ten men and continued to meet regularly, usually on a weekly basis. These groups were called "I Groups," with the letter "I" representing the "Integration" into their lives of the weekend lessons.

These groups became like a band of brothers that dove deep and shared issues, experiences, and victories. Many of these groups have remained intact over the years.

A large portion of the New Warrior process was inspired by Gestalt Therapy, which involves play-acting, role-playing and expelling bioenergetic energy, which is intended to bring to life or clarify hidden issues. This work is called "shadow work," a paramount idea in Jungian psychology. Typically, these were hidden issues affecting men's lives.

One practice involved "going under the blanket." In this exercise, a man would lie on the floor cloaked by a blanket, a metaphor for being in the grave. Men would hold the blanket down, the man forced to face the issue keeping him in that "dead state." He would have to fight his way out, back to life, so to speak, and his bioenergetic victory would or could be paradigm-shifting for him.

Each night, at our meetings, we would sit in a circle and "check-in," which was an opportunity for each man to be fully present with the other men. Part of the check-in process included each member declaring, "If I were to work tonight, here is what I would do." Then, the man would say either, "I chose to work tonight" or "I choose not to work tonight."

When my turn arrived, I was engulfed by a dark and foreboding feeling. As if someone else were commandeering my voice, I uttered, "If I were to work tonight, I would get under the blanket." Of course, I ended up on the floor, smothered by a blanket held firmly in place by some of the men in the circle.

I woke to find myself in a grave with my father, my grandfather, and my uncle. Although I was chronologically in my mid-fifties, under that blanket, I felt as if I was a young boy again. Then, I found myself standing over my father's casket while that pastor asked me if I wanted my father's ring.

One of the men facilitating my work asked me what I wanted. This time, I responded, "I want his ring." The men scrambled around the room and mustered up a wire keychain ring, which they slipped on my finger.

The effect of that little ring on my finger was astonishing. I didn't have to fight my way out of the grave, I almost levitated up and out of it. Atlas' burden for me – the weight of the world that that little boy carried over the tragic deaths of those three men – lifted from his shoulders. The hidden guilt and responsibility he carried for all those years dissipated into the ethers.

Tears poured out, but finally, they were tears of relief and joy. I found myself in an altered state of transformation that only Jesus himself could provide.

I went home that night and confided in my sweet Suzi what happened. She bubbled with excitement and happiness for me, inquiring in detail about the ring. I told her that I did remember it: a weathered, silver Indian head ring.

What I didn't realize was that Suzi was conspiring with my men's group, and they made me a silver Indian head ring in my size. The group soon presented it to me as a "token" for my work, another tremendously moving experience.

When a man completed his weekend experience, he received a leather thong, a talisman, to commemorate his "initiation" into a new era of manhood. Many men added other items that held personal significance to them.

I always wore my talisman when leading each New Warrior Weekend experience. My ring was on my talisman, and often, men would ask me about it. I'd tell them the story of the ring that represented my father's blessing. I'd offer to let them hold the ring, to feel their own fathers' blessings.

My journey working with hundreds of men over the years was very eye-opening. So many never received their father's blessings, leaving a mortal wound inside of them. My father's ring became a powerful metaphor that seemed to help open a transformational healing gateway for many of them.

And as my own journey continued, my eyes kept widening. I realized that although it is so fundamental for young boys to internalize that "you have what it takes" message, the true eternal blessing, received only by our heavenly Father, matters the most.

This message, too, can come from strong, Holy Spirit-filled fathers who model and communicate Christ-filled living and blessings.

Chapter 14

Moving on with Men

*Standing With the Redwoods
and Emerging from Plain Sight*

Following my exit from the now-named Mankind Project, I embarked on a sort of wilderness experience. I spent volumes of time at my church discussing men and men's work and ministry, but nothing tangible seemed to come from it. The church itself struggled to determine what to do for men, but these conversations led to nothing substantive.

Doesn't this seem like one of the eternal stories in the modern-day church? Many murmurs and small, isolated events, but rarely does one find a community of faith with dedicated staff and resources targeted toward specifically nurturing ongoing, life-changing men's ministry.

One day, while writing about this on Facebook, a message popped up from an old Warrior brother with whom I had lost contact: "Come and staff a Crucible Weekend with me."

I had never heard of the Crucible Project. However, he quickly introduced me to a couple of their leaders, who welcomed me with open arms.

This group had been around for many years, and, as it turned out, it was modeled after the New Warrior Weekend. Same protocols and processes, but Crucible diverged in being Christ-centered, with lots of prayer and Scripture. The group is blooming exponentially with a current global presence. Coincidentally, or perhaps not, they held some of their Texas weekends at The Land Of My Grandfather.

After men finish initiation weekends in this group, they continue to meet in small groups called "Soul Groups." They call themselves "Redwoods," in iconic reference to the massive strength of the giant redwood trees, which possess shallow roots, yet build support by bonding underground with surrounding trees.

Similarly, we as individuals do not have the strength to weather every storm alone, but by fusing with our communities and leaning on the Lord, we build deep, protective roots. What an incredible metaphor.

Crucible leaders are strong, God-fearing men, and it has been, and remains, a blessing to get to know them. I highly recommend the work they do for men.

Chapter 15
All Roads Lead to the Sad State of Modern Men

There are other Men's Ministries stepping up to empower, heal, and energize men to become living examples of Christ-centered, godly masculinity. One of these incredible groups is called Thumos, originating from the Ancient Greek concept of "spiritedness."

Thumos is founded and led by a man whom I've personally worked with and mentored in prior men's groups. Jody Licatino is a brave, visionary who left a corporate career to launch this ministry in faith. The following is a quote from ThumosUSA.com: "We are a connected community of real (not perfect) men, made up of husbands, veterans, young men, retired men, church members, corporate employees, business owners, etc., but all are committed to being better and helping each other live full lives via coaching and mentoring. Thumos was created to help men win. These men build more, do more, look better, feel better and are better. We are building better men."

I am also familiar with the Illuman (Illuman.org) men's ministry founded by the well-known author, Father Richard Rohr. An American Franciscan priest and ecumenical teacher on spirituality based in Albuquerque, New Mexico, Rohr is a prolific writer and founder and leader of the Center for Contemplation, which "seeks to empower individuals to live out their sacred soul tasks in service to the world through contemplative programs and resources."

Healthy Male initiation and Rites of Passage

Through all these years of learning, healing, leading, and teaching, I have come to demystify the core phenomena of these men's ministries and movements. Though some of these groups did not explicitly use this language, what each strove for, albeit through their own methods and processes, was essentially initiating men into a new way of manhood.

Chapter 16
Initiating Men into a New Way of Manhood

Father Richard Rohr addresses the concept, practice, and imperative societal role of men's initiation in his article, "From the Archives: Why Men Need Initiation" published in the October 12, 2020 edition of *Today's American Catholic*. Rohr writes:

> The whole thing that got me into this work of understanding initiation was my observation of the state of the male of the species, both clergy and layman. We are not in good shape! We tend not to naturally understand spirituality. In fact, I am convinced that the male is naturally resistant to its essential language of intimacy, surrender, patience and trust. Men like roles instead of processes, dressing up instead of dressing down.

As a Senior Leader and facilitator of men's work for almost 30 years, Rohr's comments track with my own observations and experiences regarding men's initiation.

Ancient cultures considered the initiation of a young boy into mature adult manhood essential to the ongoing survival of their community. Typically, a mother raised her son during his early years. Eventually, men in the village would snatch the "Momma's boy" away. While initially petrified and both boy and mother wailing, once the boy left, the mother would settle down, have coffee with her friends, and rest in the expectation that, "My little boy is gone, but a man will return!" Meanwhile, the fearful boy would find himself in the woods, endure a challenging ordeal, survive, and then enter a circle of elders purposefully training boys into mature men.

Elements of rites of passage include the following:

1) *Retreat*: Go away, leave the comfort of mother's care

2) *Ritual*: Experience an ordeal, potentially deadly or death-like, that involved fighting personal demons, overcoming fears, lighting shadows, or even healing wounds.

3) *Return*: With the support and encouragement of a circle of initiated men and elders, return to the world changed from a boy into a man.

In Joseph Campbell's 1949 book, *The Hero with a Thousand Faces* (Pantheon, 1949; New World Library, 2008), he theorized that myths worldwide share a fundamental structure he called "the Monomyth" that consists of seventeen stages summarized in three phases: Separation, Initiation, and Return.

Jesus experienced similar rites during his death, burial, and resurrection. He further implied his disciples (initiates) would experience them personally, too, when he said, "The cup that I drink you will drink, and with the baptism with which I am baptized, you will be baptized" (Mark 10:39).

Many in our society, including the church, have lost the appreciation of earned wisdom, transformative experiences, and the importance of male initiation. I believe, along with Rohr and others, that these types of rites of passage are an innate necessity for any culture, especially for the Church.

Young men left to themselves regularly create unhealthy and unsafe initiations for each other, such as during college fraternity or street gang initiations. But young men can benefit from individually edifying and societally constructive initiations with guidance and wisdom from older sages.

During the 1980's and 90's a flurry of powerful men's work took place. These included movements like Promise Keepers – started in 1990 by Bill McCartney, Head Football Coach at the University of Colorado Boulder. Patrick Morley's *The Man in the Mirror: Solving the Twenty Four Problems Men Face* (Wolgemuth & Hyatt Pub, 1989; Zondervan, 2014) became one of the 100 most influential Christian books of the 20th century. Robert Bly's *Iron John: A Book about Men* (Addison Wesley, 1990; Da Capo Press, 2015), and Joseph Campbell's *The Hero's Journey* (Harper San Francisco, 1991) alluding to the journey within became a key marker for many of these men's groups, including the New Warriors.

But this "men go deep and wide" version did not seem to gain traction in many churches because, in my opinion, church leaders (clergy) and lay men were unwilling or afraid to "trust the process" and "surrender" to the depth and painful reality of emotional suffering, death, and resurrection.

Many churches essentially emphasize training clergy and laity to appropriately ascend the organizational hierarchy. Safe, marketable programs target religious consumers. No spiritual retreats, no wilderness experiences, no initiation pathways, and no safe spaces. The busy consumer doesn't have time anyway, so church attendance with a little Bible study thrown in satisfies the market niche.

As Rohr writes, "We Christians heard it from Jesus to Peter: 'When you were young, you put on your own belt . . . but as you grow old, somebody else will put a belt around you' (John 21:18). There have always been two life tasks for men. We teach the first easily and understandably, but very few teach the second, even in the Church. Maybe because they have not been initiated and made the descent themselves. They are still putting on their own belt. What I am saying is that we desperately need real 'elders.' And when they get there, they cannot keep retiring to Florida."

There are two elements worth noting in the recent history of men's work. One is the fading way of elders who know that, through the grace of God, wisdom gained through their journeys through brokenness led them to a state of joyful transformation. The second is the recognition and awareness of the absolute transformational power of the Holy Spirit. Experiential, not intellectual, this inner journey can lead to a person's new birth, often described as being "born again." This is none other than the light after the darkness, the joy of resurrection, joy of being, and the truth of personally experiencing the Gospel of Jesus Christ.

But as Rohr says, "Now when the Church itself stops believing this—its own Gospel—the Spirit teaches it quickly elsewhere. Presently, men in AA groups, women in cancer survivor groups, and early orphaned children often believe this more than many clergy."

Over almost 30 years of men's work, as I helped lead male initiation rites for thousands of men, I became aware of a problematic double-edged sword. Despite palpable, real, and true transformation in many men, lack of a healthy church home in which to grow and mature in the faith and experience ongoing sanctification by the Holy Spirit often allows life's busyness, recreation, work, and myriad other things to sidetrack BECOMING men from BEING new men.

Rohr concludes, "Like all liminal and sacred space, Male initiation restores an Absolute Center, Called 'GOD,' and that of course, relativizes everything else. No wonder perhaps that the Church itself is eager to forget it."

Tears of Sorrow, Tears of Joy

Chapter 17
My "Romeo Group" and What They Have Meant to Me

A divine treasure of this stage of my life has been yet another group of men which has been meeting for many years. It started as a classic small men's group. We indulged in Bible Studies and other studies, intertwining our lives together in so many ways. I am the oldest member of the group. Most men are in their seventies, and we have one "youngster," Chuck, who just hit sixty. But don't let his youth fool you; Chuck is a wonderfully spiritual man.

I have been blessed with generally excellent health. I have had some gastrointestinal issues and was once described by my doctor as "an extremely young eighty-three-year-old male with issues." One of my friends joked that this was good for my ego. Perhaps it was, but I consider my robustness to be a blessing. It is such a joy to be God's man at this point of life.

People frequently voice that I don't look my age. To this, I laugh, "You can't see my infrastructure!" I house lots of corrosion in this body: artificial hips, spinal fusion, and so on. But the pump is still working well, the pipes are clear, and the control system, my brain, still appears functional.

I attended a water aerobics class at my local YMCA. The group included a couple of men and around twenty-five older ladies. During a discussion about our ages, when I shared my involvement with my group. One of the women chuckled, "Oh, you are in one of those Romeo groups."

I stared blankly at her, not comprehending her joke. When I asked her to explain further, she responded, "Retired Old Men Eating Out!" Our group erupted in a fit of laughter. I agreed, responding, "All we talk about is our health. Joe just had a hip replacement, Tom is getting a colonoscopy, and so on."

"Oh, I call that the organ recitals," the lady giggled. Such grand fun, getting older. Good humor goes a long way.

My group has been such a joy in my life. It is well-known that one of the keys to living well is to maintain fulfilling, close relationships with others. This is vital. And I'm fortunate. My "Romeo" group has become a meaningful streamline of support and blessing, growing in magnitude as the ministry has evolved.

I am eternally grateful to Richard Selke, Ron Dagley, Blair Lerner, Chuck Nelson, Brien O'Brien, and Bill Massey for so many years of sharing lives and growing in faith together. God bless each of you!

Chapter 18
"Wake-Up Call," Formerly Known as "The Daily Seedbed Text," and J.D. Walt

One man in my group, Richard Selke, is a treasured friend, truth teller, and brother. His earthly presence aside, Richard is a true brother in Christ. He is a retired Methodist pastor and a profound teacher of the Word. And one afternoon, he introduced us to the teachings of J.D. Walt.

It has been from J.D. Walt that I learned the profound and true reality of the Holy Spirit of Jesus, including the fruit and gifts of the Holy Spirit. I have been a Christian all my life, yet it took a long time for me to become fully aware of the truth of the Holy Spirit for believers. This revelation has profoundly transformed me in the best of ways, and I have experienced a rebirth, as if I were a new child, and joyfully share this truth wherever I go.

Later in this book, I lay out the incredible impact this awakening can have on believers of all ages. It was also J.D. Walt who validated the opportunity that exists among the elder body of believers, and his teaching that helped lead to the manifesto outlined in the next chapter.

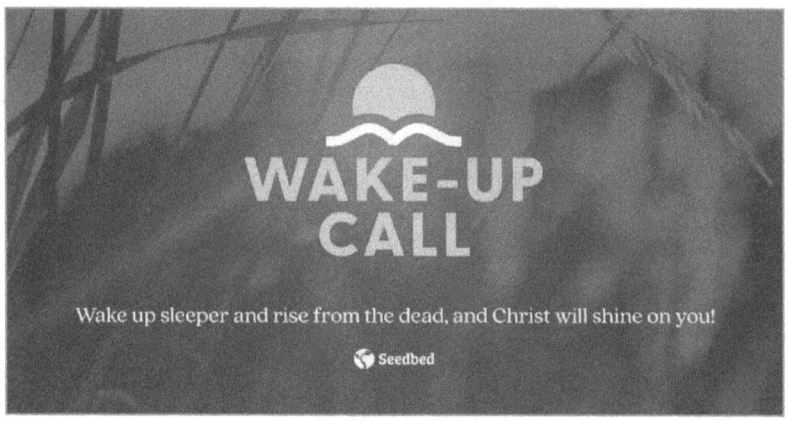

Wake-up Call by J.D. Walt is a daily encouragement to "shake off the slumber of our busy lives and turn our eyes toward Jesus. Each morning our community gathers around a Scripture, a reflection, a prayer, and a few short questions, inviting us to reorient our lives around the love of Jesus that transforms our hearts, homes, churches, and cities." For more information, visit Seedbed.com.

In addition to spiritual nurture through his writings and friendship, J.D. has ingrained in me a "spiritual practice" to greet people as follows, "The spirit of Jesus in me greets the spirit of Jesus in you and brings us together to the Father and the Son and the Holy Spirit. Amen!"

Chapter 19

Crown of Glory: A Manifesto for Christian Spiritual Eldership

"Gray hair is a crown of glory. It is gained in a righteous life."
(Proverbs 16:31)

Today's America hosts a vast army of millions of mature Christian spiritual warriors, hidden in plain sight by the modern church and by society itself.

There are older men and women who are and have been seed planters germinating their families, their workplaces, their neighborhoods, and their communities. These gardeners have watched their seeds of faith bloom and grow in the spiritual maturity of others. They love to feed the hungry, not only the physically hungry, but also those who hunger for knowledge, wisdom, faith, and a personal relationship with Jesus. These people form the earthly hands and feet of Jesus, serving the less fortunate among them in ongoing and tangible ways. They embody the call to "Love your neighbor."

They are the storytellers among us who frame their unique and rich life stories within the Grace of God. These are their personal testimonies of faith.

Reflecting on his own entry into the realm of elder saints in the church following his 55th birthday, J.D. Walt offered this perspective:

> Local churches are confused about old people. They think we want to fold bulletins, go on museum tours, and attend seminars on aging, and I almost forgot, write checks. And it's time to stop grouping us into triaged ghettos of the progressively aging. The world trends toward gathering and grouping people according to their inabilities and incapacities. Because the Kingdom of heaven is ontologically distinct from the world, the Church Jesus is building must be categorically different. Everywhere you find the Church Jesus is building it will reveal a DNA of intergenerationally, unearthing a culture of spiritual parenting and grandparenting. (Excerpt from "I Would Like To Welcome Me To The Elder Class," April 12, 2022, *Wake-Up Call*, Seedbed.com.)

Fertilized by this concept, the Crown of Glory Fellows Ministry was born with the intentions to:

- Encourage, activate, and inspire Christian spiritual elders.
- Encourage modern churches to invite and create time, space and resources for spiritual eldership and teaching.

Our globe's elderly Christians cannot and should not have to force their way into the church's eye. The church ignoring the golden-aged demographic in terms of resources, programs, and worship and Bible study services is downright neglectful and catastrophically irresponsible. It appears our nation has forgotten the spiritual wisdom gained through aging under the Lord's shepherding hands, and it isn't our elders' obligation to issue this reminder.

This tremendous problem is best solved when our elders are energized by the church itself. They must be invited or enlisted to present themselves, and then encouraged to pour into the lives of the people they serve.

Over the last several decades, our culture has gravitated increasingly toward youth worship and elder rejection. Elders have become increasingly invisible. It has been said that for the godless progressive worldview to prevail, the wisdom of the elders must die out. This trend is indicative of a falling, sick, and confused society.

Alarmingly, the modern church has responded to this issue by compounding it. The church continues pouring enormous resources into youth programs, while turning away from the elders. Nurturing our youth is beautiful, appropriate, and a crucial need. Yet, despite the church's efforts to steer youth, we continue to lose our fresh faces to the culture.

Could it be time to enlist that Hidden in Plain View Army of Christian Spiritual Elders?

Mine is a passionate plea, a clarion call to intentionality and strategic action, for the church Jesus is building to tap into the DNA of intergenerational community. Together, we can unearth the culture and unleash the power of spiritual parenting and grandparenting.

> To the elders among you, I appeal as a fellow elder
> and a witness of Christ's sufferings who also will share
> in the glory to be revealed: Be shepherds of God's
> flock that is under your care, watching over them—not
> because you must, but because you are willing, as God
> wants you to be; not pursuing dishonest gain, but
> eager to serve; not lording it over those entrusted to

you, but being examples to the flock. And when the Chief Shepherd appears, you will receive the crown of glory that will never fade away. In the same way, you who are younger, submit yourselves to your elders.
(1 Peter 5:1-5 NIV)

Amen!

Chapter 20
God: The Great Dot Connector

One matter of which I have become increasingly aware as I continue to ride the earth ship around the sun is how God keeps connecting these endless "dots of our lives."

Take, for example, the fascination I once had with the demographics of aging in our population. I finally found the connection.

The Mission Field for Christian Spiritual Eldership

I found the following demographics in a government population project I read somewhere back in 2019:

The Silent Generation
  Ages 77 – 91, 23 million, and decreasing rapidly.

Baby Boomers: Children of the Silent Generation
  Ages 58 – 76, 72 million, and declining slowly.

Gen X: Children of Boomers and Grandchildren of Silents
  Ages 39 – 57, 72 million, and declining very slowly.

Millennials: Children of Gen X, Grandchildren of Boomers, and Great-grandchildren of Silents
  Ages 23 – 38, 72 million, and becoming the largest.

These populations, scattered and blended throughout the world, encompass a massive mission field. It's essential, as Christians, to engage in worldwide mission trips and touch unreached souls. Yet we have a huge mission field (340 million people) right here in our homeland as well.

Let's analyze the Boomers. This generation, our youth's parents and grandparents have been described in endless ways. They are categorized by many unique virtues, some beneficial, and some not great and consequential. It is important to note that, as a rule, the priorities and elements they cherish are equally valued by their children.

Boomers have been described as the wealthiest, most self-interested, and most consumerist generation. They direct great focus and energy into wealth and wealth accumulation, safety and security, leisure and travel, and increasingly, health and retirement.

My circles are mostly populated by people of this generation, and they frequently ask, "What shall I do with myself now that I have more time and money? What is my purpose?"

In America today, I believe that this group is the fertile mission field for Christian spiritual eldership, both as seedbeds and seed planters.

They are familiar with the song, "Is that all there is?" And they have enough life experience to respond, "There but for the grace of God...".

Due to the sheer number of people in this cohort, the market has risen for many "retirement ministries." We are experiencing a growing realization that retirement is an American capitalist idea, but not a definitive biblical mandate. Examples include Finishing Well Ministries and Retirement Restoration.

The dire need for life purpose post-retirement plays out in many useful ways, as seen in programs like retirement counseling, career counseling, and life coaching. Each has tremendous value in helping people navigate an ever-changing world and their own ever-changing lives.

But if we want to create a vehicle for truly transformed spiritual eldership, perhaps the best term to use would be "recovery."

Envision a Center for the Recovery of Christ-Centered Spiritual Eldership. The program would aid in recovery from our worldly addictions to:

- Money and wealth
- Power
- Control
- Leisure
- Sports
- Cultural idols and idolatry
- Political idolatry
- False safety and security
- And, in later years, health issues

In addition, we are warring against epidemic-level societal addictions to vices such as pornography and drugs. We know that addictions are largely attempts to cover up internal wounds and pains unique to each addict. "Recovery" is a process designed to heal those wounds.

Today, the U.S. hosts a diverse population of about 340 million people. We regularly witness clashes between radically opposing worldviews, compounded and accelerated by the Internet and the 24-7 news cycle. This phenomenon has sparked countless movements with the term "great," including "The Great Reset" and the "Great Awakening."

"Great" has become a term synonymous with someone's solution to the world's problems.

Perhaps it is time for a "Great Recovery" in which we come to our knees for Jesus and pray for what only the Great Healer can provide through our surrendering to Him. He embodies the only true transformation into a new life, filled with the fruits of the Holy Spirit.

The recoverable history of spiritual eldership in Christianity is powerful. The metrics speak for themselves. In the Old Testament, elders were revered heads of households, crucial leaders of tribes and rulers within communities. In the New Testament, elders transcended into the roles of spiritual overseers and earthly shepherds of the church.

The book of Revelation reveals that the Lord appoints twenty-four elders in heaven to lead His people through Jesus Christ when He begins His eternal reign (Revelation 4:4, 10; 11:16; 19:4). Yet, today, elders are systematically dismissed, ignored, and left to wither away, wisdoms untapped, by the broader society, and more harmfully, by many churches.

As I ponder elder roles, I'm left with a lingering question: Is it possible that a new center for the recovery of Christian spiritual eldership could become a seedbed for His purpose?

> "Teach us to number our days, that we may gain a heart of wisdom." (Psalm 90:12)

> "In that day the Lord will reach out his hand a second time to reclaim the surviving remnant of his people." (Isaiah 11:11)

> "The Spirit of the Lord is on me, because he has anointed me to proclaim good news to the poor. He has sent me to proclaim freedom for the prisoners and recovery of sight for the blind, to set the oppressed free." (Luke 4:18)

> "Wake up, sleeper, rise from the dead, and Christ will shine on you." (Ephesians 5:14)

Chapter 21
It Only Took 82 Years of Being a Christian to Reach a Complete Understanding of the Holy Spirit of Jesus in Me

I have always been a Christian. Although my parents died when I was young, as I grew up, I came to understand that they planted two foundational messages in my brain.

One: "Son, you have what it takes!"

Throughout my very crooked path, this underlying belief gave me courage and a strong sense of adventure. While my journey continues and my story is still being told, this notion helps maintain my unconditional confidence during this "Crown of Glory" phase of my life.

John Eldredge's book, *You Have What It Takes: What Every Father Needs to Know* (Thomas Nelson, 2007), exhorts fathers to plant seeds of confidence in their sons. I dedicated years to working with men through the healing of deeply embedded "you are not good enough" injuries often inflicted by unconscious, wounded parents. When we come to embody the Holy Spirit of Jesus in us, we are more than good enough in His eyes. This message is incredibly, deeply therapeutic.

Two: "God is real, and Jesus loves you."

Looking back, my understanding was simple, confined to the limitations of a young boy's growing mind. Yet the effects of this message were lasting and profound. Years appeared and faded and the world constantly challenged me. I clung to these words for comfort, never really doubting them.

I've always been involved in church, and my sweet Suzi and I have been churchgoers throughout our marriage. Most of our children attended church as well.

As a leader by calling, I've held many roles in our different churches. I've served in church councils, a pastor parish committee, a finance team, in small group ministries, and in many other positions. My wife and I have benefitted from great anointed preaching, and I've been blessed to have attended men's retreats and trained hundreds of men.

I earned a Bible Seminary certificate after a rigorous eight semesters of classes and endured an intensive ten-month Colson Fellows Program.

And yet, I still was not fully aware of the truth that the Holy Spirit of Jesus resided in me. This revelation, albeit simple, is intangible and difficult to fully internalize. So many of us know this without fully knowing this.

I remained in a state of half-comprehension of my blessing until I was eighty-two years old.

I once wrote, on the white board in my office, "Holy Spirit come!" Ironically, I wrote this as if the Spirit was out there somewhere, rather than within me.

My mindset astronomically shifted when J.D. Walt entered my life. My new outlook has surely transformed me in so many ways: from how I think, to how I feel, and what I do.

No longer do I ask, "What would Jesus do?" Now, I question, "What is Jesus doing through me? Right now? Right here?" And now, I am sitting at a small keyboard, pouring out the truth of the Holy Spirit. Amen, and thank you Jesus!

Chapter 22

Awakened Wedding Vows

Incredibly, I was blessed to officiate at the weddings of two of my grandchildren and of my youngest son, David and his sweet Sarah. The evolving awakening of the Holy Spirit within me was reflected in the vows of each wedding.

The first wedding I officiated was that of our beloved granddaughter, Michaela, and her man, Mac. It was an intimate outdoor wedding, high up in the splendid grandeur of the Rocky Mountains. Their union was biblical and so special, overlooking the epic backdrop of the Lord's creation.

The second wedding was of our son, David, and his Sarah, on a beautiful beach in Isla Mujeres, Mexico. This gorgeous destination is one of our favorite spots in the stunning country. It drastically differed from the Colorado wedding, yet it was also biblical and deeply special.

The third wedding was of our grandson, Brant, and his lovely Jen, a couple of years later, in Austin Texas. Prior to their union, I had endured a radical period of growth. God had been developing my understanding of the Holy Spirit, and this is reflected in their vows, included herein with permission.

Tears of Sorrow, Tears of Joy

Michaela and Mac Smiley, August 22, 2021

Sarah and David, October 31, 2021

Brant and Jennifer Goss, *December 10, 2022*

Tears of Sorrow, Tears of Joy

Nuptial Ceremony for the Holy Matrimony
Brant Goss and Jennifer Scott
December 10, 2022
Austin, Texas
Officiant, Stanley B. Goss

Officiant: "Who gives this woman to be wed?"

Father of the bride: *Dr. John William Scott III, M.D.*

Officiant

The spirit of Jesus in me greets the spirit of Jesus in you and brings us together to the Father and the Son and the Holy Spirit. Amen.

We are gathered here today, before friends, family, and above all, God, to witness the Holy Matrimony of Brant Goss and Jennifer Scott.

We thank the Lord for all the blessings that brought us here today, and those that brought Brant and Jen together, to make this day possible.

And we are thankful for the blessings of another day with our loved ones, and especially grateful for this day when we can be around friends and family, some of whom have traveled great distances to be here.

Love and marriage is truly one of God's greatest gifts and accomplishments. Yes, the heavens and the earth are pretty impressive, but the Lord has filled us with love and allows us to grow that love exponentially by sharing it with someone else. And so, by giving selflessly to another, we make ourselves stronger and our lives that much richer. Marriage is one of the greatest miracles we have been given.

So, Jen and Brant, it has been so much fun to watch, over the last year, this amazing event being created. So much planning, so many details: venues, food, decorations, flowers, gifts, showers, bachelorette, and bachelor parties.

I acknowledge your planner, Katie, for her loving and brilliant guidance. Such brilliance, creativity, and goodness everywhere. All culminating today, in a reunion of people who have come to love and celebrate you.

And as beautiful as it all has been, it is of the world and in the world; once married, you will continue to live in the world.

But your desire is to be wed in Holy Matrimony. Holy means spiritual, it is not a worldly condition,

So, let's go there now. As your spiritual faith grows individually and together, you will experience a Holy Transformation through the spirit of Jesus in you.

As Jesus said in Matthew 19, "Therefore a man shall leave his father and his mother and hold fast to his wife, and the two shall become one flesh. What therefore God has joined together, let no man separate."

So, it is time to bring the fruit of the Spirit into this moment.

According to Galatians 5:22, "But the fruit of the Spirit is love, joy, peace, patience, kindness, goodness, faithfulness, gentleness, and self-control. Against these things there can be no law."

So Brant, would you say to Jen:

Jen, I bring you love.
I bring you joy. Joy is love rejoicing.
I bring you peace. Peace is love at rest.
I bring you patience. Patience is love waiting.
I bring you kindness. Kindness is love interacting.
I bring you goodness. Goodness is love initiating.
I bring you faithfulness. Faithfulness is love
    keeping its word.
I bring you gentleness. Gentleness is love empathizing.
And I bring you self-control, which is love
    resisting temptation.

And Jen, would you say to Brant:

Brant, I bring you love.
I bring you joy. Joy is love rejoicing.
I bring you peace. Peace is love at rest.
I bring you patience. Patience is love waiting.
I bring you kindness. Kindness is love interacting.
I bring you goodness. Goodness is love initiating.
I bring you faithfulness. Faithfulness is love
   keeping its word.
I bring you gentleness. Gentleness is love empathizing.
And I bring you self-control, which is love
   resisting temptation.

And so, to live according to God's will, we have the Holy Spirit within us; the Word of God before us in the Holy Scripture; and the interceding Jesus above us, who providentially works on our behalf. Amen.

So, it is time.

Brant, do you promise to love, honor and respect Jen above all others, from this day forward, until your very last day on earth?

Jennifer, do you promise to love, honor and respect Brant above all others, from this day forward, until your very last day on earth?

May I have the rings please?

These rings represent love, pure and simple. The love God has for all creatures, great and small, and the love you, Brant and Jennifer, have for each other. When you place that ring on your partner's finger, know that you are giving not just the gift of a ring, but also the gift of love the Creator has filled you with.

Brant, please repeat after me,

Jen, please accept this ring as a token of my true pure love for you. With this I give you my heart and soul. They are yours forever more.

Jen, please repeat after me,

Brant, please accept this ring as a token of my true pure love for you. With this ring I give you my heart and soul. They are yours forever more.

We thank God for bringing Jennifer and Brant together. I am so personally blessed to have shared this with you. Now, by the power vested in me, I pronounce you man and wife. You may kiss the bride!

Beginnings are important. So important that the term is the first noun in the Bible, which says, "In the beginning..." What follows is the heavens and the earth, water, life, man, woman and marriage. Although you have known each other for a couple of years, from this day forward, your lives will never be the same. You have a great beginning, Brant and Jen. Now, it is up to you.

Begin each day together with fresh love, and you will enjoy an amazing married life together!

Ladies and gentlemen, I present to you,

MISTER AND MRS. GOSS!

Chapter 23
From Practical Atheism to Spirit-Filled Christian Spiritual Eldership

Earlier in this book, we explored the manifesto and mission for this ministry. It seems apparent now that throughout these past several decades, I would argue since the 1960s, we have witnessed a devastating downturn in the number of "faith based" people in our country.

The following statistics are staggering:

- In the 1980's, 75% of our population self-proclaimed faith and considered themselves "believers."
- This dropped to under 60% by 2020.
- Soon, this number is expected to drop to under 50%, with the trend most extreme in our younger generations.

In the following chapter, I cite an article by John Stonestreet, President of The Colson Fellows Center. In his brilliant piece, he describes the concept coined "Practical Atheism."

Chapter 24
'Signals of Transcendence' in a World of Practical Atheism

*For many in the modern West,
life proceeds without even considering God.*

By John Stonestreet, *Breakpoint*, 03/29/23

Reprinted with permission from The Colson Center for Christian Worldview (Breakpoint.org/signals-of-transcendence-in-a-world-of-practical-atheism/)

Many Christians, a college buddy of mine once observed, are "secularists with a twist." They believe in God and hope to go to heaven when they die, but they live lives that are largely indistinguishable from everyone else. Secularism is, after all, the default way of thinking about life and the world in our culture: It is the water we swim in, the air we all breathe.

In his book, *The Way of the Modern World*, author and theologian Craig Gay described this pervasive everyday secularism. The problem, he said, isn't that most people are atheists, because they are not. Though more people, especially in rising generations, identify as non-believers and religiously unaffiliated, a red-blooded atheist is still hard to find in the wild. The most common thing we encounter, Craig Gay wrote, is "practical atheism." In other words, what shapes our world is not so much a proliferation of people who believe that God does not exist; rather, it is that so many people live as if God does not exist, as if God is irrelevant to most of life.

Secularism, in other words, has not been nearly as successful in disproving faith as it has been in dismissing faith. Within a secular framework, faith is relegated to the realm of the personal and the private, irrelevant to larger questions about reality or truth.

In his monumental work, *A Secular Age*, philosopher Charles Taylor argued that the marginalization of religious belief has led to the "disenchantment" we experience in the modern world. While the sacred aspects of life and reality were plain and obvious to prior generations, those who have been shaped by the ideas, technologies, and habits of a modern world tend to miss the sacred, the transcendent, and the Divine.

Scripture's metaphors also make little sense to most in a disenchanted culture. As practical atheists, we can grow deaf to the heavens' loud proclamation about the glory of God. Stars and rainbows remind us of human achievement and self-authentication, not of God or His promises. Even breathtaking events like weddings, the birth of a child, and death itself fail to point our hearts and minds upward and outward. Instead, we can become trapped in the here and now, in what Taylor called the "immanent frame."

In other words, we live in a world where the assumptions that govern how we think and what we do are almost always secular ones. For many in the modern West, life proceeds without even considering God. Good things come from our hard work and planning, not from the gracious hands of our loving Father.

Practical atheists are, in this way, at constant risk of idolatry. As John Calvin said, humans are incurably religious creatures, and a secular age offers all kinds of God-replacements: sex, self, stuff, state, and science. A secular age is, ironically, filled with faith...just in all the wrong gods.

One way that Christians can intentionally swim against the secular currents in today's culture is to constantly look for and point out those indications of God that He has placed in the world about Himself. God has infused His world with glimpses and reflections of His character and His grace, experiences that can wake us from our secular stupor. In God's common grace, a stubborn sense of discontent, an unresolved question, a deep sense of some foundational truth become profound gifts to draw people outside of themselves to the eternal. He has, as the author of Ecclesiastes stated, "put eternity into man's heart."

In a new book, author and social critic Os Guinness calls these "signals of transcendence." In it, Os tells of 10 individuals who sought God after a moment of joy, beauty, comfort, or failure. The remarkable stories told in *Signals of Transcendence* are a profound testimony of the power of God to invade the hearts and minds of even the most stubborn secularists. And thank God, He did. Otherwise, we may never have known the blessings of *Narnia* and *Middle Earth*, among other things.

Signals of Transcendence: Listening to the Promptings of Life is a profound tool for living and pointing others to Christ in a time of practical atheism. It will sharpen your own senses to find a God who is present and active in the world He has made. Receive a copy of *Signals of Transcendence* for a gift of any amount to the Colson Center this month. Just visit ColsonCenter.org/March.

For more resources to live like a Christian in this cultural moment, go to ColsonCenter.org.

Tears of Sorrow, Tears of Joy

Chapter 25
How Now Shall We Live Our Crown of Glory Years?

The Word on the Crown of Glory

"Therefore, my brothers and sisters, you whom I love and long for, my joy and crown, stand firm in the Lord in this way, dear friends!" (Philippians 4:1 NIV)

"Now there is in store for me the crown of righteousness, which the Lord, the righteous Judge, will award to me on that day—and not only to me, but also to all who have longed for his appearing." (2 Timothy 4:8 NIV)

"Blessed is the one who perseveres under trial because, having stood the test, that person will receive the crown of life that the Lord has promised to those who love him." (James 1:12 NIV)

"When the Chief Shepherd appears, you will receive the crown of glory that will never fade away." (1 Peter 5:4 NIV)

"Be faithful, even to the point of death, and I will give you life as your victor's crown." (Revelation 2:10 NIV)

"Gray hair is a crown of glory; it is gained in a righteous life." (Proverbs 16:31 NIV)

Chapter 26
Complete Your Understanding of the Holy Spirit and Embody the Transformation Within

Ken Boa, in the introduction to his great book, *Life in the Presence of God: Practices for Living in Light of Eternity* (IVP, 2017), includes the following invitation:

> I hope I can convince you that becoming more conscious of God's moment-to-moment presence is something that you need and can have. It's an innate capacity that every true believer has and can cultivate. From the time a person first believes (is born again), God puts his Holy Spirit in every believer (Pentecost) and that Spirit is now available to us every second of every day. (p. 3)

If you read Romans 8:11, Corinthians 3:16, and Ephesians 1:13-14, you can read the Word supporting this assertion.

Alarmingly, most Christians live largely unaware of this divine presence. This state of blindness leads to our detriment and impoverishment. Moreso, we remain sightless at the risk of being disobedient to the commands of Jesus (see John 4:8).

As J.D. Walt regularly exhorts in *Wake-Up Call*, "Wake up, you sinners, and arise from the dead. Let the Spirit of Jesus shine on you and through you."

In C. S. Lewis' classic book, *The Screwtape Letters* (The Centenary Press, 1945), Screwtape writes to Wormwood, "Humans are amphibians—half spirit and half animal...As spirits they belong to the eternal world, but as animals they inhabit time" (p. 44).

Boa's book includes these comments on that perspective:

> Great Christians know this kind of living. C. S. Lewis said that humans are sort of "amphibious beings." Frogs are amphibious because they can survive on land or in water. They're able to live in water, but they also hop on land. We're not amphibious from a biological standpoint, but we are from a spiritual one. Like frogs, we live in one world, while belonging to another. We can be with the God of heaven while our feet are firmly planted on earth...We can train ourselves to embrace our amphibious nature." (pp. 25-26)

Chapter 27
Prepare for Training

"Train up a child in the way he should go; even when he is old he will not depart from it." (Proverbs 22:6)

"If you put these things before the brothers, you will be a good servant of Christ Jesus, being trained in the words of the faith and of the good doctrine that you have followed. Have nothing to do with irreverent, silly myths. Rather train yourself for godliness; for while bodily training is of some value, godliness is of value in every way, as it holds promise for the present life and also for the life to come." (1 Timothy 4:6-8)

"He also told them a parable: 'Can a blind man lead a blind man? Will they not both fall into a pit? A disciple is not above his teacher, but everyone when he is fully trained will be like his teacher.'" (Luke 6:39-40)

"Solid food is for the mature, for those who have their powers of discernment trained by constant practice to distinguish good from evil." (Hebrews 5:14)

"For the moment all discipline seems painful rather than pleasant, but later it yields the peaceful fruit of righteousness to those who have been trained by it." (Hebrews 12:11)

"I saw that under the sun the race is not to the swift, nor the battle to the strong, nor bread to the wise, nor riches to the intelligent, nor favor to those with knowledge, but time and chance happen to them all." (Ecclesiastes 9:11)

"Do you not know that in a race all the runners run, but only one receives the prize? So run that you may obtain it." (1 Corinthians 9:24)

"Therefore, since we are surrounded by so great a cloud of witnesses, let us also lay aside every weight, and sin which clings so closely, and let us run with endurance the race that is set before us, looking to Jesus, the founder and perfecter of our faith, who for the joy that was set before him endured the cross, despising the shame, and is seated at the right hand of the throne of God." (Hebrews 12:1-2)

Chapter 28
Have the End in Mind

Commit to the Marathon Called Life

In Boa's book, *Life in the Presence of God: Practices for Living in Light of Eternity* (IVP, 2017), he articulates the training processes and "spiritual practices" integral to one's life journey. I've listed the highlights of these processes and practices below.

- Re-do everything. Life, as you currently understand it, must radically transform.

- As followers of Christ, our entire faith is based on the prefix "re-."

    - *Resurrection*
    - *Revival*
    - *Reconciliation*
    - *Repentance*
    - *Restoration*

- Boa suggests training in the following "Re-" spiritual practices:

    - *Rewiring Your Mind*
    - *Re-seeing the World*
    - *Reorganizing Your Time*
    - *Rejoicing Amid Suffering*
    - *Repenting of Sin*
    - *Remaining in Community*
    - *Reimaging Life*

Chapter 29
Your Life IS Your Ministry

Making it Real

As you read the *Wake-Up Call* by J.D. Walt reprinted in the next chapter, consider reflecting deeply on this paragraph:

> We are coming to the close of a period of Church where the general understanding has been that one had to be a minister (read, clergy) in order to have a ministry. Clergy did the 'ministry' and the laity helped around the edges when needed. This model still prevails in a lot of places, but it does not resemble the church envisioned by the New Testament.

Tears of Sorrow, Tears of Joy

Chapter 30
Why It's Time for You to Enter the Ministry

By J.D. Walt
Wake-Up Call, May 30, 2022

COLOSSIANS 4:17

Tell Archippus: "See to it that you complete the ministry you have received in the Lord."

CONSIDER THIS

I wonder if Archippus was there when they read the letter. Was he on the proverbial fence as to whether he would fulfill his calling? Was he waiting on a word from the Lord? A lot of people are.

Here are the deets on Archippus. We have it on good evidence he was a preacher in Colossae. There's pretty good evidence he went on to be the bishop of Laodicea. He is also referenced as a "fellow soldier" in Paul's letter to Philemon (v. 2 NRSV).

So beyond that, what do we do with a verse like, "Tell Archippus: 'See to it that you complete the ministry you have received in the Lord'" (Col. 4:17)?

I've got an idea. Try this.

Tell [insert your name here]: "see to it that you complete the ministry you have received in the Lord."

You have one, you know—a ministry. In the original Greek language, the word for ministry means, "to wait tables." Think about the last time you were at a restaurant where a waiter or waitress served you. In the biblical sense of the term, they were ministering to you. Where in your life do you find yourself waiting tables as it relates to serving other people?

We are coming to the close of a period of church history where the general understanding has been that one had to be a minister (read, clergy) in order to have a ministry. Clergy did the "ministry" and the laity helped out around the edges where needed. This model still prevails in a lot of places, but it does not resemble the church envisioned by the New Testament.

You have a ministry. Maybe you've not understood it as such. Maybe you've thought of it as just doing good or doing the right thing or as a civic duty. What if it could be raised to the level of Jesus? What if that ordinary act of service, of waiting tables, could be charged with the energy of the Holy Spirit? The task would still be ordinary, but your touch would carry transformational power through doing it.

Maybe you have a ministry at the local assisted living center? Maybe your ministry is in your work as a lawyer or a doctor or a checker at Wal-Mart. Maybe your ministry is as a crossing guard at an elementary school. Maybe you have a ministry of being Santa Claus during the Christmas season. Perhaps your ministry is driving elderly people to the doctor who can't drive themselves.

Whatever it might be, what would it mean to raise it to the level of Jesus? It would mean at least two things. First, it would mean lowering your stature in the sense of your willingness to take on lower and lower tasks. Second, it would mean raising the level of spiritual power in your service. You are responsible for the first step. Jesus will take care of the second. We see this marvelously at play when Jesus washed his disciples' feet.

"See to it that you complete the ministry you have received in the Lord" (v. 17). It's probably a good word we want to start speaking to each other too.

THE PRAYER

Abba Father, we thank you for your Son, Jesus, who came not to be served but to serve. Give me fresh eyes to see the possibilities to minister to others "in the Lord." We pray in Jesus' name. Amen.

THE QUESTIONS

1. *Have you ever thought of yourself as a minister? Why or why not?*
2. *What is your ministry? How do you wait on tables?*
3. *What might it look like for your ministry to be raised to the level of Jesus—to go lower in stature and higher in power?*

For the Awakening,

J.D. Walt
Sower-in-Chief
Seedbed.com

Tears of Sorrow, Tears of Joy

Chapter 31
Starting over with Grace

Aging Gracefully

Many years ago, probably in the early 1970s and while working in Los Angeles, I attended a workshop hosted by motivational speaker, Charlie "Tremendous" Jones. I recall that he said many inspirational things during that one-day workshop. Out of these, my mind reduced his words to a single "aha" nugget which I have carried with me for years:

> *The number one skill in life is this;*
> *be very good at 'Starting Over.'*

This ancient truth and wisdom has served me well over the decades, and I have shared it with countless people as a means of reflection and conscientious living.

In truth, doesn't that sum up much of life? Everything changes. Everything has a beginning, a middle, and an end.

God knits us together in the womb, we exit into the world outside, and then find ourselves immediately "starting over."

We grow from infants into young children, often living in a sheltered, cloistered environment, and then start over again.

We move on and mature through kindergarten, then move on to the next level and start over again.

The cycle continues – grade school, junior high, senior high, college, career – our lives chronologically categorized into multiple eras of starting anew. Change is inevitable, and we are constantly required to start over.

For a long time, I experienced many, many losses: deaths of family and friends, personal divorces, personal financial ruin, business failures, and sixty-two jobs.

I also found a vehicle for boundless personal healing and transformation of my deep childhood wounds.

At the age of fifty-two, I answered a latent calling I had since childhood, and over the next twenty-five years created and led a multi-million-dollar leadership coaching practice.

My seventies were my most productive years. My business flourished. God moved me to intently study His Word. Following His calling, my studies at The Bible Seminary and with the Colson Fellows better equipped me to defend and articulate the true biblical worldview.

In recent years, I manifested two personal ministries: Crown of Glory Fellows and Love your Neighbor.

The truth for me now has never been clearer: Jesus is the answer. My salvation through Him is astonishing. This is the ultimate proof of God's Grace, a supernatural power, in the earthly realm, and in me.

So, our natural lives are cyclical, routinely consisting of countless periods of starting over and continuous cycles of change from beginning to end. This way of living is perhaps best described in Ecclesiastes 3, which begins, "There is a time for everything, and a season for every activity."

Every cycle comes to an end, and the best path to starting over is to forge a fresh, exciting, and new beginning.

We do not always get to choose our beginnings or endings. Some are painful and entail personal loss. Some are forced upon us. But as we grow and mature, especially emotionally, we develop resilience, and with this strength comes courage.

With change comes faith, or perhaps, with faith comes change. And as we journey through life, we can become bolder and more intentional about where we go next.

It is easy to relate in terms of our worldly experiences. We all have unique stories. Fluxes and shifts in relationships, schools, educational choices, career changes, losses, financial statuses, physical locations, illnesses, achievements, and so on are universal human experiences.

By the eighty-fourth year of my journey, I concluded that I got here and became the person I am due to the undeserved grace of Almighty God. There is a supernatural reality to life on earth that has become more and more real to me as I have matured, both physically and spiritually in my faith walk and relationship with Jesus.

In earthly terms, eighty-four years is a long time: 30,681 days. At this stage of life, each day is a tiny fragment of my life. This only reminds me to see each day as a gift and to spend the time well. From an eternal perspective, each day is another step toward my Heavenly Father.

The author of the biblical book of Ecclesiastes, most likely the ancient nation of Israel's wise King Solomon, famously researched numerous things in life and wrote a summary of his actions, conclusions, and reflections. He repeatedly claimed that "M*eaningless, meaningless!*" things included money, power, and human philosophy. He warned that life, at its best, is all but vain without remembering our Creator, fearing God, keeping His commandments, and keeping in mind that all will be judged.

Countless lives throughout history have confirmed those assertions. Wisdom, pleasure, alcohol, human achievement, great riches, and sex all lead to "vanity" without a proper relationship with God.

The author ends Ecclesiastes with these words:

> "Now all has been heard; here is the conclusion of the matter: Fear God and keep his commandments, for this is the duty of all mankind. For God will bring every deed into judgment, including every hidden thing, whether it is good or evil." (Ecclesiastes 12:13-14)

The Bible weaves the big story – the eternal God, all creation, sin and redemption, justice and mercy, and the Messiah – throughout stories of numerous individuals across thousands of years. As we read their stories, we learn more about our own stories and the countless events that comprise our lives. Genesis to Revelation sheds light on both the natural and supernatural realms and affirms that our stories as believers will continue into an eternal future. Ultimately, the story of Jesus is the roadmap for us all.

I claim the call and legacy given to me by the Lord. I believe that God's grace permeates my human interactions not because of what I have made myself to be, but through the ways God has shaped me by the power of His Holy Spirit throughout my lifetime of stories.

Seek and you shall find...grace.
Look and you shall see...grace.
Listen and you should hear...grace.
Open your heart and you shall feel...grace.

Wake up sleepers and arise from the dead!

Chapter 32
Grace, A State of "Bee-ing"

Seeing God's Grace in All Things

The date was March 10, 2020. The paramedics estimated that I had over one-hundred bee stings on my swollen, excruciating body. Agonizing red marks painted my head, face, neck, hands, and arms. My ears, nose, eyebrows, and lips, brutally stung, had begun to inflate. I'd suffered so many stings that the paramedics resorted to scraping the stingers off my body with a credit card.

On a scale of one to ten, my pain was about twelve. I was in a state of utter shock, dazed, bewildered, panicked, and screaming in pain.

Yet like most stories of human experience, this is a story of God's grace.

When it Happened

It was Tuesday morning at 11:10 a.m. I had just returned from a post-back surgery consultation with my doctor, neurologist G. Alexander West. A few months prior, on January 16, Dr. West had performed a micro-laminectomy and fusion on my lower back. My recovery was going well, and the doctor cleared me to return to normal activities. Little did I know then that my return to "normalcy" would only last an hour or so! And not just mine, due to the horrendous bee encounter I was about to experience, but everyone's, since America's Covid-19 pandemic began that very same week.

Where it Happened

Our neighborhood is a quaint, quiet enclave of one-story patio homes. We live on the west side of our street, which hosts a long row of homes that backs up to the Meadowbrook Farms Golf Course, a beautiful, par five dogleg-right hole. A very large sand trap is located directly behind our house.

Because our homes are on the golf course, each lot is segmented by open, black wrought iron fences, instead of the conventional, cedar wood fences common to most homes in the region. We enjoy stunning views of the course. We also have a gate from our backyard onto the course, one of the few gates along the fence line.

The Cast of Characters

Michelle

Facing the golf course, Michelle and her husband, Ron, reside in the house to our right. They have been our neighbors for many years. They are Canadians, and each in their 50s at the time.

Michelle is a self-proclaimed "green" environmentalist, who adamantly opposes chemicals in her garden, whether it is fertilizer or bug spray. She loves bees due to their vital role in pollinating the plants of the world. Because there is so much information circulating about the endangerment of bees, Michelle is particularly sensitive about protecting them as much as possible.

Aside from their garden, Ron and Michelle have a pool in their backyard. They are very good neighbors, and my wife and I are quite fond of them. We consider Michelle a kind, generous and caring woman.

Joseph

We didn't know his name at first, so I refer to him as the "Golf Course Worker."

Colin

If one stood at our fence, facing the golf course, Colin lives three houses to the left. A white-haired, retired oil industry executive of Irish or Scottish descent, Colin "just happened to be in his backyard" as this story began to unfold.

Suzi

My wife of forty-four years at the time of publication, Suzi is my sweetheart, my yoked-in-Christ partner, who just so happens to have a severe bee allergy.

Layne

Layne is the general manager and head pro at the golf club. He is an old friend of mine, although we don't interact much anymore due to my back issues, which have prevented me from playing golf for several years. We are like-minded Facebook friends who frequently share quips, grandkid stories, and political commentary.

The Incident

I arrived home from my doctor's visit an hour or so before and was about to head to the front door to join some of my neighborhood friends in our weekly "Sandsage Sages" lunch.

Suddenly, Suzi cried out that something was wrong with the Golf Course Worker. Shortly prior, the man was driving a large mowing tractor back and forth along our fence line. Suddenly, he stopped the tractor right between our house and Michelle's, jumped off, and began running around, screaming, and waving his arms wildly.

Suzi's account stopped me in my tracks, and I immediately rushed outside toward our back gate to see what was going on. My eyes scanned the fence line to the left, where I saw the worker now standing and talking to Colin, who had been in his backyard.

I unlocked the gate, stepped out onto the course, and began walking down to talk with the two men. As I stepped onto the course, I became acutely aware of a loud, buzzing sound circulating my head. Initially, I thought I'd attracted an annoying insect and tried to swat it away. This mistake was lethal.

Instantly, a large swarm of angry bees attacked, engulfing my head. Moments later, I began to feel the indescribable pain of their stings. I panicked, thinking I could escape them, and bolted out past the sand trap. But the swarm followed me, and the noise and pain intensified.

They relentlessly stung the top of my head, inner ears, face, eyebrows, and even my lips. As I tried to fight them off, they fought back, counter-attacking my hands and arms. I tore off my white, Duke Blue Devil "family" shirt in an aimless attempt to beat the black-and-yellow army off, but to no avail.

Later, when Suzi took my shirt to the laundry to wash it, dead bee bodies fell off from all over the inside and outside.

I staggered, and collapsed into a fetal position, barely able to move. The pain I succumbed to was otherworldly. It was at that point that I heard the faint beckoning of Michelle's voice, saying, "Stan, Stan get up and come with me."

By then, I was in a hazy state of shock and surprised to find that Michelle there. I didn't know where she came from or why she was beside me.

Later, I learned how that came to be. Like Suzi, Michelle heard the tractor driving back and forth along the fence. Recalling that the bees dwelled in a tree in her backyard, she ran out to warn the Golf Course Worker. But, by then, he had already been attacked. He quickly dismounted the tractor, and, having seen Colin out in his yard on his last pass with the tractor, darted toward him.

But as Michelle stepped toward her fence to warn the worker, some of the bees attacked her. She, too, was swarmed and stung. She had been talking on her cell phone with her business partner, who told her to jump in her pool and call 911, which she did. She then jumped out of the pool and dashed back through her house and out the front door. Ron, her husband, was in his office on a business call, and had no idea what was happening.

Michelle then ran through our backyard, telling Suzi what was happening. Then, she sprinted through our unlocked gate and turned left, painfully aware that Joseph, the Golf Course Worker, had been injured and was seeking refuge with Colin. But Michelle hadn't known I was out on the course. Within the same couple of minutes, Suzi took our dogs inside the house and picked up a towel with a plan to come out and rescue me.

By then, Michelle heard me out on the course and traveled those seventy yards or so with her own towel in tow to save me. She has a vivid recollection of a moment while we were on the course during the attack of a brilliant butterfly flitting by. The bees attacked the butterfly and destroyed it in seconds.

Incredibly, Michelle somehow got me back on my feet. We staggered toward the others. My memories of these final events are cloudy, but when we were a few feet away, I've been told that Joseph hoisted me up by my belt and dragged me the rest of the way.

I'm unsure if Colin was actively watering before, but as we approached his house he directed his hose toward Michelle and I in an attempt to wash the angry legions of bees off our battered bodies.

So, there we stood, the four of us. Three bee sting victims and a wise-eyed Colin, hosing us down, and unsure how he'd ended up playing hero. I'm sure I was in shock, partly from the pain, but largely from the anaphylactic shock from all of the bee venom. My body was in full blown response to that.

The EMTs arrived almost immediately. I learned later that there were three teams and three ambulances. They had to find a way over Colin's fence to reach us on the other side, as he didn't have a gate. I'm not sure how they did get over it, but I've retained a clear memory of a red-headed medic kneeling beside me, offering me assurance, and competently administering aid.

The medic started treating me first, in part due to my age, and partly because he speculated that I had the most stings. He estimated that I received over a hundred stings, potentially a lethal dose for someone over eighty years old. I recall him scraping endless stingers off my arms, hands, ears, eyebrows, face, and lips with a credit card.

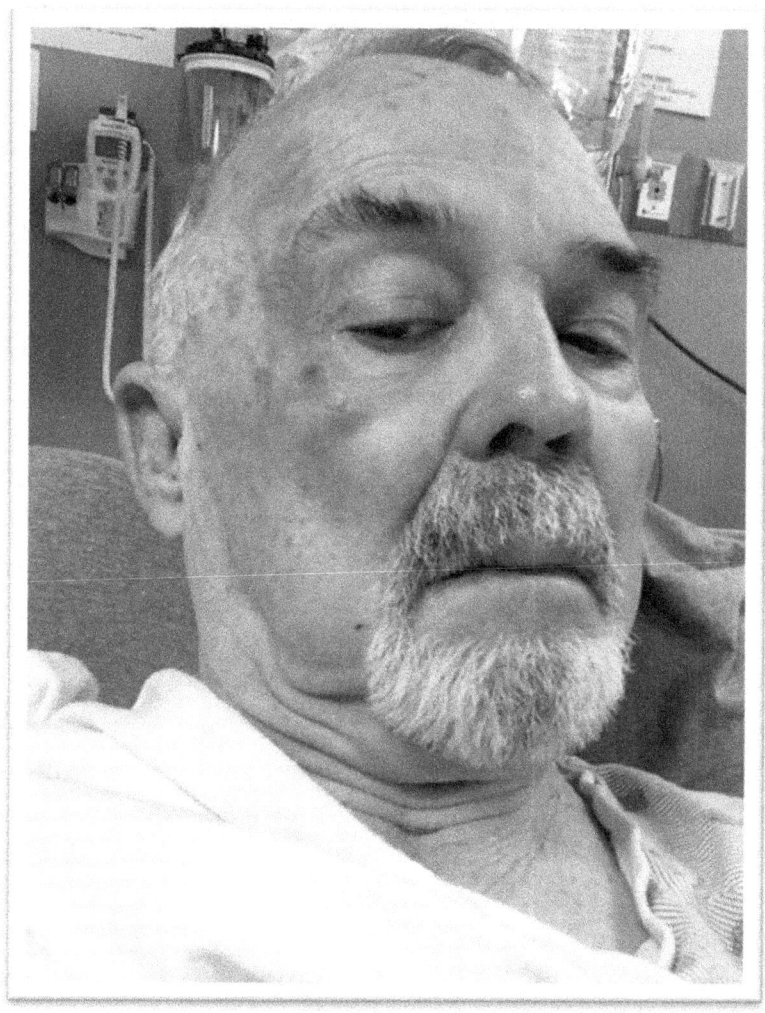

He immediately injected an EpiPen in my thigh. He also injected me with Benadryl and inserted an IV to prep me for the "emergency room" portion of the journey, which included steroids, more Benadryl, another antihistamine, and most crucially for me, a morphine drip for the pain.

Yet the obstacles weren't over. The next challenge for the teams of EMTs was getting us off the golf course and into their ambulances. The nearest gate was at our house, but their assessment of the path indicated far too many grudge bearing bees continued to swarm that area.

So, they did what they had to do. The EMTs went to their well-equipped ambulance and returned with the saw that they needed to cut out a section of poor Colin's fence! In came the gurneys, and the other victims and I were promptly rolled out to the street, into the ambulances, and less than ten minutes later into the Emergency Room at Memorial Hermann Katy Hospital. What a fantastic place staffed by fantastic people!

Because of my circumstances, they rushed me straight to an examination and treatment room. Meanwhile, Michelle and Joseph remain stationed on their gurneys in the hall. It took about fifteen to twenty minutes for my morphine drip to begin to take effect and the intense pain began to lessen a bit.

As noted earlier, these events coincidentally, or perhaps not, unfolded on March 10, 2020 – the first day of the widespread U.S. Covid-19 protocols. The hospital had just initiated screening procedures, so Suzi and Ron, Michelle's husband, had to go through screening. Eventually, the hospital staff met us and Michelle and Ron were able to visit the room I was in. Joseph remained in the hall for a while until he was admitted for an overnight stay.

By this point, Michelle and Joseph were very sick and vomited. Thankfully, that didn't happen to me. They kept Michelle and I in the hospital for four hours of observation, then discharged us with prescriptions for EpiPens, steroids, and two types of antihistamines.

A lasting consequence, reiterated by medical personnel, is that we are now highly sensitive to bee stings. Michelle and I, per medical counseling, must carry EpiPens and Benadryl at all times. In fact, they told me if I am ever stung by a bee again, even once, I should self-inject and immediately phone 911. With one sting now equal to one hundred, the threat of future anaphylactic shock is very prominent.

Michelle called professionals that night to remove the bees. The procedure took a little longer than anticipated, since the bees remained agitated until after 8 PM.

What a story! This had the makings of a real-life drama, brimming with surprise, shock, pain, fear, heroism, and foremost, grace.

Michelle was flooded with remorse throughout this event. She knew the bees were lodging in her tree for some time, and liked it, believing she provided a safe harbor. However, she lacked the foresight to realize the danger that her hive posed to neighbors and other unwary passersby like Joseph.

Recognizing the burden that Michelle carried, I visited her the next morning. She was overflowing with emotions: relief, pain, fear, and the heavy cross of guilt. I shared with her that there was grace in this story; she witnessed what unfolded and learned a hard lesson.

I told her, "We are Christ followers. As such, we are forgiving people." I yearned to help lift the burden from her back, much as Jesus lifted those heavy burdens from us.

Sherds of Grace

Occurrences are anything but random. There are so many notes of grace, and their perfect, timely intersections, that I've pinpointed in this story.

The sheer fact that Colin was in his backyard, and that Joseph saw him, was amazing. Because of his hose, and the washing of bees that came with it, lives may have been saved. Since I began to verbalize this story, I have heard several times of people having died from such lethal stings.

With Suzi heading toward the course to save me and her serious allergy to bee stings, without Michelle arriving on scene, there may have been a lethal outcome for sweet Suzi Q.

While the EMT administered aid to me, he uttered this, "I love bees. They are my favorite animals on the planet. Without them pollinating the earth, we would not be able to eat the way we do. They just don't belong in your backyard." I'm not sure where Michelle was at that moment, but I'm fairly sure he was talking to her.

Michelle, upon hearing me out on the course, had the courage and compassion to come and get me and drag me toward the hose, despite the ongoing bee attacks upon her. This was absolutely incredible.

The following day, I drove over to the Golf Course Clubhouse. I felt an urgent need to lay my eyes on Joseph, whose presence during the event was a dim blur to me. After all, he was the man whom I went to check on at the outset, and also the man, I learned, who picked me up by the belt and dragged me through my final distance to the water hose.

Upon my arrival, I found out Joseph was taking a couple of days off, and that my friend and his boss, Layne, was out on the course. Staff called him, and he came to see me.

It was pleasant to see each other and share the bee drama. But then, the conversation took a heartwarming turn. Layne revealed that he thought of me often. For many years, a core concept of my Leadership Coaching practice was the essence of "mastery." In fact, my business name was The Mastery Group. Several years prior, Layne had invited me to come over and share these principles with his staff.

Layne shared with me that he adopted these concepts and integrated them into his work and life. He was grateful. This, for a master, coach, and teacher, is the greatest reward: to see seeds you have planted bearing fruit through others. This is grace. Led by bees back to a reconnection with Layne.

I told Layne one of my greatest motivations for my then-recent back surgery was to be able to play some golf again. He was very encouraging, and offered to introduce me to some other eighty-year-old golfers who would welcome me to enjoy the game with them. This, too, is grace!

A couple of days later, when Joseph returned to work, Layne brought him to the house. As we stood by the gate and shared our stories, we experienced deep healing together. This is also how grace works.

I now see Colin almost every day out in front of his house. I've told him before that I will never see him in the same way. This is grace.

Suzi, Michelle, Joseph, and I have experienced a real ordeal together. We survived. We are closer because of it. This, too, is grace.

James, in his exhortations to the early followers of Christ, framed it this way:

"Consider it pure joy, my brothers and sisters,
whenever you face trials of many kinds, because
you know that the testing of your faith produces
perseverance. Let perseverance finish its work so that
you may be mature and complete, not lacking anything."
(James 1:2-4)

Steadfastness. Perfect and amazing grace!

Tears of Sorrow, Tears of Joy

Chapter 33
Age, Eldership, and the Sage

Learning to look for wisdom in today's elders

"Gray hair is a crown of glory; it is gained in a righteous life." (Proverbs 16:31)

"The righteous flourish like the palm tree and grow like a cedar in Lebanon. They are planted in the house of the Lord; they flourish in the courts of our God. They still bear fruit in old age; they are ever full of sap and green, to declare that the Lord is upright; he is my rock, and there is no unrighteousness in him." (Psalms 92:12-15)

"Do not rebuke an older man but encourage him as you would a father, younger men as brothers, older women as mothers, younger women as sisters, in all purity." (1 Timothy 5:1)

"So I exhort the elders among you, as a fellow elder and a witness of the sufferings of Christ, as well as a partaker in the glory that is going to be revealed: shepherd the flock of God that is among you, exercising oversight, not under compulsion, but willingly, as God would have you; not for shameful gain, but eagerly; not domineering over those in your charge, but being examples to the flock. And when the chief Shepherd appears, you will receive the unfading crown of glory. Likewise, you who are younger, be subject to the elders. Clothe yourselves, all of you, with humility toward one another, for "God opposes the proud but gives grace to the humble." (1 Peter 1:5)

The Stage of a Man's Life, Called "the Sage"

The following quotes are excerpts from John Eldredge's book, *Fathered by God: Learning What Your Dad Could Never Teach You* (Thomas Nelson, 2009, pp. 198-204).

> I am old enough to be scripturally dead. I want this possible extension of life to be hard as always, but also new, something not done before: like writing stories, or preaching or discipling others. This is the heart of the Sage: to make his greatest contribution with the last years of his life. At this stage a man's kingdom may be shrinking. But his influence should actually increase. A Sage differs from an expert the way a lover differs from an expert.
>
> The Sage communes with God – an existence different from and utterly superior to the life of the expert. Whatever counsel he offers, he draws you to God, not to self-reliance.
>
> Our culture in the progressive West has dismissed the elderly for years now, because we have worshiped adolescence. This is why we have a world now of uninitiated men. Thus the heart of the Sage is wounded

when he is dismissed or sent to exile or Scottsdale – which is pretty much the same. No one seems to want what he has to offer and he comes to believe after a time that it is because he has nothing to offer.

It is important that we ask, because often in humility the Sage will not offer until he is invited to do so. It is also important that we ask quite often, because the Sage himself is not aware of all that he knows. It is the question that stirs his soul; his memory as a smoldering fire leaps to life again when stirred. In this way we can help to raise the Sage.

Tears of Sorrow, Tears of Joy

Chapter 34
How Sowing Seeds Builds the Kingdom of God

There are fifty kernels in one head of wheat and up to seventeen thousand kernels in just one pound. The kernel is the seed from which the wheat plant grows.

Because I spent my youth on a dryland wheat and dairy farm in eastern Colorado during the post-Depression and World War II era, I naturally experienced the hands-on learning process of the relationships between man, earth, plants, and animals.

We grew most of the food we consumed. My family and I kept a freezer stocked full of home-grown protein: beef, pork, and chicken. Our eggs were the real deal, fresh from the nest. We managed a herd averaging forty dairy cows, drank some of the milk, and sold the bulk of it for additional income. As a small child, I learned to hand-churn butter and ice cream. We cultivated a huge garden and canned enough vegetables and fruits to last through winters. We supplemented our reserves with cherries and peaches from regional orchards.

Our primary source of income came from an annual crop of winter wheat. We planted each fall, and the wheat grew throughout the winter, flourished in the spring, and ripened by summertime.

During the harvest, crews of Texans with fleets of wheat-cutting combines rolled through, tracking the south to north cutting seasons. Prayers aplenty arose each year for successful cutting and storing of the wheat crop into storage silos in town. Notorious and seemingly whimsical Colorado summer hailstorms could destroy crops in a matter of hours.

This lifestyle helped me learn the value of hard work and responsibility at an early age. I fed chickens, gathered eggs, slopped hogs, and milked cows twice a day.

Grandma regularly sent me out to catch a couple of chickens for dinner. I would grab each chicken by the neck and spin them around until the bodies separated from the heads in my bare hand. I then plucked the feathers and delivered ready-to-cook chicken to Gram. It was a fragile relationship, the dynamic between man and animal.

I left the farm and farming in my early teenage years. But these hands-on life experiences no doubt played a major role in my understanding of the teachings of the Bible, especially the Gospels. To this day, I am an avid gardener. I regard time in the garden as my "God time." I want the great hymn, "In the Garden," played at my celebration of life.

I still stand in awe of how God, our Great Creator, can transform a miniscule seed into an eggplant, or a tomato, or a beautiful rose or plumeria. Truly, we have an awesome God!

Much of America has ceased living at an agricultural level. No longer a people of the soil living in intimate proximity with the new life and fruitful death cycles of plants and animals, we have transitioned from farms and factories to an information-based, technologically driven society. Work-worn hands no longer routinely cultivate soil. Fewer people pray without ceasing for provision and protection while patiently waiting for God's seeds to miraculously multiply crops they planted.

I have no doubt that for the last few generations, including the youth of today, this plays a factor in their ability or inability to relate Biblical teachings, parables, and stories to their physical reality. This may also explain the great drift in our contemporary world between the heavily populated urban centers and the geographical center and mid-west and south where agriculture remains a prominent way of life.

Jesus routinely integrated common gardening concepts into his teaching. He used agricultural metaphors: Sowers, wheat fields, fig trees, mustard seeds, vineyards, vinedressers, branches, garden laborers, seeds, barren trees, and the life cycle of plants.

Agriculture was both a way of life for Israel and a welcome sign of God's covenant blessing. Enjoying the Lord's fruitful provisions indicated that He continued fulfilling His promises to Abraham in successive generations. Even the spiritual, intangible concept of "the fruit of the Holy Spirit" is rooted in the physical, tangible realities of a bountiful creation.

The Bible integrates copious animal kingdom references: sheep and goats, flocks and shepherds, fish and fishermen, bears, birds, bulls, camels, lambs, lions, wolves, and serpents all comprise key elements in the Gospel story.

The proof of the impact of spiritual seed sowing is found in stories recounting the multiplication of seeds planted in faith. Facilitated over the years through my coaching practices and ministry, I experienced abundant blessings that include many, many stories of how seeds were planted, grew, and multiplied through others.

I'll confide in you a few.

Alix

Several years ago, I was engaging in a Bible study with my fourteen-year-old granddaughter, Jordan, her sister, Emily, and several of their young friends.

One of the girls, Alix, posed to me this question, "Pa, my Sunday school teacher told us that if we didn't go to church every week that was a moral sin. What do you think?"

The Holy Spirit prompted me to say, "That might be church dogma, but it is not biblical. My source of truth and inspiration is the Bible and the Gospel of Jesus Christ."

Alix allowed this seed to root. She became an avid student of the Bible and a devoted follower of Jesus. She has pursued a path through college and missionary work and now serves on the staff of a fast-growing church in Austin, Texas.

Suzi and I attended Alix's wedding celebration recently, and I reminded her of this Holy Spirit moment. She recalled it vividly and told me it brought her goosebumps. A life-changing seed of faith planted within her long ago led to Alix becoming a seed sower herself.

Mika

I met Mika twenty years ago at a men's group training. We lost contact, but his face recently popped up on my Facebook page due to connections through a couple of mutual friends. Through them, I heard he and his wife were strong believers and involved in powerful ministries within their church.

I reached out and we arranged to meet for breakfast. There, Mika revealed that when he stepped foot into that men's training, he arrived as an atheist. He ran with a fun-loving, party group and attended at their invitation.

I was a leader then, and Mika told me that my quiet and persistent position as a Christ-follower made an impression on him. In some small way, our encounter that weekend cracked open a door of faith into his heart. Mika is now a big-time seed sower in his own right.

Melanie

My wife and I once received a holiday card, which read as follows:

Dear Stan,

I was glad to come across an online article you authored in *Katy Christian Magazine*. It reminded me of working with you many years ago when I was at Chase. I still recall some of the sage advice you gave me and even share some of it with others on occasion. One that sticks with me right now is your guidance that there are 3 important factors in your career satisfaction – whether you love the work you do, the people you work with, and the values of your organization. It was helpful to me 20+ years later in my decision to change jobs. I just wanted to let you know that you've made a difference in my life. I hope you and Suzi are well and enjoying all God has planned for you.

With gratitude,

Melanie

This practical expression of gratitude and rich reward of seed sowing is one of the purest forms of joy.

Suzi

My beloved Suzi is a talented seed sower, particularly with our grandchildren. She regularly hosts "Coffee with Nana" through which her quiet, calm wisdom and Christ-loving counsel has proved life enhancing for them.

Stan Goss

The Sower's Creed*

I sow for a great awakening.
Today,
I stake everything on the promise of the Word of God.
I depend entirely on the power of the Holy Spirit.
I have the same mind in me that was in Christ Jesus.
Because Jesus is good news and Jesus is in me,
I am good news.
Today,
I will sow the extravagance of the gospel.
Everywhere I go and into everyone I meet.
Today,
I will love others as Jesus has loved me.
Today,
I will remember that the tiniest seeds become the tallest trees;
That the faith of right now becomes the future of
The everlasting kingdom.
Today,
I sow for a great awakening.

"No one born of God makes a practice of sinning, for God's seed abides in him; and he cannot keep on sinning, because he has been born of God." (1 John 3:9)

* Excerpted from *Still Day One: Living in the Day after the Day of Pentecost*, by J.D. Walt, Seedbed, 2023. Reprinted with permission.

Tears of Sorrow, Tears of Joy

Chapter 35
Disturb the System, Make Waves, Be Bold and Fear Not

*I may be getting older,
but I'm not going out quietly!*

Isn't it a tragedy that the older we get, the more afraid we become? All our life experiences should have pointed us in the opposite direction. Most of what we feared at various points never happened. This alone should have shattered our mental barriers of fear, yet how many times have we regretted not stepping into a perceived risky scene?

In her book, *The Four-Fold Way: Walking the Paths of the Warrior, Teacher, Healer, and Visionary* (HarperCollins, 1993), Angeles Arrien brilliantly captures the "warrior way" as a four-step process:

1. *Show Up* – Where is the place, event, or situation that calls to me?

2. *Be Fully Present* – Be unafraid, non-angered, and unsad. Just be. Experience life with a full presence.

3. *Seek and Speak the Truth* – This is the biblical sword of truth. Completing this step may prompt an emotional response. The truth will set you free, but it very may hurt feelings or make someone mad. The fear of an emotional response is the primary reason most choose to stay silent or keep the truth to themselves. Are you willing to step into that vulnerable, exposed place, or do you just "play it safe?"

4. *Accept the Outcome and Walk On* – This is the way of Jesus, the Peaceful Warrior. He showed up. And eventually, He showed up at the cross for us. In those final, agonizing earthly moments, He remained fully present to what was happening to Him and around Him. He said, "*I am the Truth.*" And He accepted the outcome, for us.

Why do we do less? *Fear.* Why should we follow Him? *Love.* I have concluded that life is a delicate dance of our navigation between love and fear. This is biblical!

There are thirty-three citations of fear in the Bible. We are encouraged repeatedly, "*Fear Not!*" We are instructed, "The fear of the Lord is the beginning of wisdom" (Proverbs 1:7).

Contemplate this: Fear is an emotion, not a fact. We house four different primary emotions: gladness, sadness, madness, and fear.

"Glad" is our desired brain condition, whether it be expressed as joy, happiness, delight or so on.

"Sad" is our reaction to the occurrences of painful losses. The human condition is brittle with these, be it death, financial devastation, divorce, or perhaps the loss of a phase of life. Working through this reaction is the process of grieving those losses, and eventually, moving on. Without honoring the transitional season of grief, we remain stuck.

"Mad," or anger, is a tool we lean upon to mask pain, or a motivating force to fight for something we're afraid to lose.

We'll discuss more about fear later.

All these emotions wax and wane within our brains. Sometimes our mental bandwidths are overwhelmed by a single emotion, demanding our attention. At other times, multiple feelings flit across our minds all at once, some cohesive, others contradictory. Other times still, these emotions fade into the background, faintly humming away.

When I discuss the brain, I like to say that to believe in God, just contemplate the human brain. Did you know that one billion neurons are compacted into that three-and-a-half-pound mass between your ears? You have more capacity in your one head than the entirety of the internet!

The left side of your brain, called the neocortex, is where logic occurs. Data is input, stored and recalled as knowledge.

The right side of the brain, called the limbic system, is where our emotional processing occurs.

For years, through my leadership trainings, I educated others about emotional intelligence, or "EQ." Surveys report that the most effective people in life and work have the highest EQ. I have carried around my medical school, three-and-a-half-pound plastic brain to demonstrate these points.

The basic objective of EQ is "mood management," the ability and awareness to shift whatever mood one is experiencing, back into contentedness and happiness.

Only recently, as my understanding of the Holy Spirit has grown, have I connected the dots between this principle and biblical truths. Once again, it seems the dots of life are endless. What the Apostle Paul labels fruits of the Holy Spirit – love, joy, peace, patience, kindness, goodness, and self-control – seems very much like EQ.

Fear is a prevalent force. What is its opposition, its complementary emotion?

Again, I'll refer to literature. One of my favorite works is a book by Stephen Pressfield, *Gates of Fire: An Epic Novel of the Battle of Thermopylae* (Bantam, 1999). Perhaps familiar to many through to the similar famous movie "300" (2006) starring Gerard Butler, Pressfield's story is a fictionalized account of the Battle of Thermopylae. In it, three-hundred Greek Spartan warriors hold off two-million mercenary army soldiers hired by Persian King Xerxes. Though miniscule in numbers, these men save the Greek state.

Hand-picked by their great leader, Dienekes, the three hundred men knew they would die, but willingly charged into battle. Dienekes converses with them about fear before they head into battle saying, "The opposite of fear is love." Although this did not originate from biblical teaching, it rings biblically true.

Let's circle back to fear. A profound truth to internalize is that fear is generally based on what could happen, not what has already occurred. Although the basis for many fears is a painful past experience that we incessantly try to prevent from recurring, our fear itself emanates from an internal concept of a prospective future, not the reality of a certain past.

Thankfully, we possess a tool for dealing with fear in a logical, rational way: risk management. In the secular world, this is a commonplace process that occurs all around us all the time. Banks use risk management to evaluate loans and investments, and insurance companies use risk management to issue policies. Emotion is supposed to be removed from these processes so that they are solely based on logic.

How could this process fit into the spiritual component of our journeys?

One, consider all the "fear not' admonitions. Ponder what they meant to the hearers when spoken and why they must have been considered important enough to be included in scripture for us to read.

Two, consider "love." The word appears nearly 700 times in the Bible. The Greatest Commandments summarize the focus and scope of love:

> "When the Pharisees heard that he had silenced the Sadducees, they gathered together. And one of them, a lawyer, asked him a question to test him. 'Teacher, which is the great commandment in the Law?' And he said to him, 'You shall love the Lord your God with all your heart and with all your soul and with all your mind. This is the great and first commandment. And a second is like it: You shall love your neighbor as yourself. On these two commandments depend all the Law and the Prophets.'" (Matthew 22:36-40)

Three, consider the fruits of the Holy Spirit:

> "The fruit of the Spirit is love, joy, peace, patience, kindness, goodness, faithfulness, gentleness, self-control; against such things there is no law." (Galatians 5:22-23)

The Glorious Conclusion

Christ conquered "death" for us. God provides everlasting "paradise" for us. Spiritually, we don't need our risk manager because the future is assured. Therefore:

> "The righteous are bold as a lion." (Proverbs 28:1)

> "They were all filled with the Holy Spirit and continued to speak the word of God with boldness." (Acts 4:31)

"(The Apostle Paul) lived there two whole years at his own expense, and welcomed all who came to him, proclaiming the kingdom of God and teaching about the Lord Jesus Christ with all boldness and without hindrance." (Acts 28:30-31)

Be like Paul!

Show up.

Be fully present.

Seek and speak the truth.

Accept the outcome and move on.

Chapter 36
The Sword of Truth

"Do not think that I have come to bring peace to the earth. I come not to bring peace, but a sword." (Matthew 10:34)

"Take the helmet of salvation, and the sword of the Spirit, which is the word of God, praying at all times in the Spirit, with all prayer and supplication." (Ephesians 6:17-18)

"Therefore repent. If not, I will come to you soon and war against them with the sword of my mouth." (Revelation 2:16)

"For the word of God is living and active, sharper than any two-edged sword, piercing to the division of soul and of spirit, of joints and of marrow, and discerning the thoughts and intentions of the heart. And no creature is hidden from his sight, but all are naked and exposed to the eyes of him to whom we must give account." (Hebrews 4:12-13)

Tears of Sorrow, Tears of Joy

Chapter 37
See the Sacred in the Everyday Rituals of Life

Dear Reader,

If you have ventured this far with me on my journey, it should be evident to you that I am, and always have been, an avid reader of books. I am an eager consumer of knowledge and wisdom. Throughout this book, I have freely passed along knowledge and wisdom that flowed from another author, into me, and now to you.

The following is another example. Robert Fulghum is a Unitarian Universalist minister and prolific writer well known for his bestselling book, *All I Really Need to Know I Learned in Kindergarten: Uncommon Thoughts on Common Things* (Ballantine Books, 1986, 1988, 2003). I devoured this book of short essays and all its insights, yet his work that affected me the most profusely is titled, *From Beginning to End: The Rituals of Our Lives*, (Ivy Books, 1996). In the preface to this book tapping into a history of human beings creating and sharing memories, Fulghum writes:

From beginning to end,
The rituals of our lives shape each hour, day, and year.
Everyone leads a ritualized life:
Rituals are repeated patterns of meaningful acts.
If you are mindful of your actions,
you will see the ritual patterns.
If you see the patterns, you may understand them.
If you understand them, you may enrich them.
In this way, the habits of a lifetime become sacred.

Is this so? I'll break down the contents of this book.

Beginning
   The rituals of our first hour of the day serve as a window displaying the life of one person. As the holy is forged out of the daily, the simple becomes sacred.

Propositions
   These are premises upon which the discussion of rituals depends, illustrated with anecdotes. The differing lines between ritual and rite of passage are crucial, as is how these ideas affect the public, private and secret levels of life.

A Cemetery View
   This beckons an answer to the question, "If you knew you had a limited amount of time to live, what would you do?"

Once
   This consists of the stories that come from asking people to continue this sentence; "I never will forget the first time I...". Thus, we participate in the ritual of remembering.

Reunion

This section details the rituals of "returning" and rites of reconciliation. We reconcile with people, things, experiences, and feelings, especially pertaining to school, family, adoption, communion, talismans, conventions, and God.

Union

The public may examine a wedding as a model of the methods by which all public rituals are observed and reformed. First, view the actual wedding, then discover a "backdrop view" of how the ceremony came about.

Born

This section describes ritualistic aspects of celebrating the welcoming of a child into a neighborhood and a neighborhood into the life of a child.

Dead

This section depicts the private observation of a funeral as a model of the ways in which death and dying are handled. First, view the actual graveside ceremony, then uncover the backstage view of how the service came to be.

Revival

This contains stories about the little deaths and little rebirths that occur lifelong on every level of existence; daily, weekly, and annually. Rituals command restoration and renewal.

Gazing at the man or the woman in the mirror

We each have morning rituals unique to us, but typically involving looking into a mirror. We go through our habits: brushing teeth, shaving, applying makeup, doing hair, and so on, all behind the stare of our mirrored reflection.

What if, one morning, we chose to look in the mirror and say, "Good morning to the Child of God?" What if we greeted our own reflection this way?

Making the Bed

At this "retired" stage of our lives, Suzi and I share most of our household chores: washing and folding the laundry, emptying the dishwasher, making the bed, and so on.

We generally share these chores or take turns. Yet, we've found that the "sacred" behind routine comes from the simple act of love and service for each other. This is rarely spoken, but constantly known and felt.

So, look around at your own life. We each must scan our various elements and involvements, be it our jobs, families, churches, or something else. With an open mind, we each will identify hundreds of mundane, everyday things. And as we begin to wake up, we will find or forge sacredness, hidden in plain sight.

Chapter 38
Taking It All to The Next Level

Finally, I will relay to you how connecting the dots of The Bible Seminary (TBS) and Colson Fellows Program led to "The Crown of Glory Fellows Ministry."

As a proud member of TBS Board of Trustees, I have communicated extensively with Dr. K. Lynn Lewis, President of TBS, and others about my vision for the Crown of Glory Fellows ministry. I hoped, somehow, to help the seminary increasingly and intentionally integrate elements of Christian spiritual eldership and sagehood into various educational and ministry experiences.

The seminary is already modeling doing so in some ways. Like me, numerous alumni and students begin seminary as part of changing careers or post-retirement. A recent alum entered the Dual Degree Completion program and graduated with both her undergraduate and graduate degree at age 70, exactly 52 years after taking her first college class and then dropping out to get married, raise a family, and embark on a decades-long career journey. She thoroughly enjoyed the learning adventure with like-minded students of all ages and stages of life and wanted to invest quality time and effort into better preparing herself for future life and ministry.

The seminary also integrates a team-teaching model that utilizes qualified adjunct faculty and other mentors who have pertinent experiences in diverse avocations and careers.

Dr. Lewis and Beau McBeth offer the following relevant encouragement in their book, *Boss Like God: A Blueprint for Elite Workplace Performance* (KL^2, 2019):

Reflection: Am I too old to do a new thing?
- Henry Ford invented the Model T at age 45.
- James Sinegal founded Costco at age 47.
- Gordon Bowker founded Starbucks at age 51.
- Ray Kroc started McDonalds at age 52.
- Ferdinand Porsche founded Porsche at age 56.
- Wally Blume founded Denali Flavors ice cream company at age 57.
- Charles Flint founded IBM at age 61.
- Col. Harland Sanders founded KFC at age 62.
- J.R.R. Tolkien published the first volume of "Lord of the Rings" at age 62.
- Laura Ingalls Wilder published her first "Little House" book at age 65.
- Donald Trump surpassed Ronald Reagan (first inaugurated at age 69) to become the oldest President of the United States at his 2017 inauguration at age 70.
- Cornelius Vanderbilt bought his first railroad at age 70.
- Anna Mary Robertson Moses ("Grandma Moses") started her painting career at age 78.
- Gladys Burrill ran her first Honolulu Marathon in 2004 at age 86 and entered the *Guinness Book of World Records* as the Oldest Female Marathon Finisher in 2010 at the age of 92.

Of course, Noah wins this entrepreneurial age contest since God seems to have called him to build the ark shortly before he turned 600 years old (Genesis 7:6). So, if you wonder whether God has a new purpose or project for you, your age might not matter as much as you think.

When Mrs. Harold Deane Akins' husband died in 1999 after 61 years of marriage, the 80-year-old knew she could have just "sat down on the couch and watched TV." Instead she prayed for a new direction that came in the form of foreign missionary work. Over the next twelve years, until her death in 2011, she embarked on a series of fruitful missionary adventures that took her around the world numerous times.

When asked, "Why?" she replied, "Just because my husband died, am I supposed to sit around and wait to die, too? No! I still have life in me, and I am going to spend it all until I am all spent!" (pp. 28-29)

The seminary offers opportunities for elders to both learn and lead on campus and online as part of classes and seminars, archaeological excavations and museum initiatives, study tours, and in writing, publishing, and productions.

The premise is that "older people," say fifty to eighty plus years old, still possess potential spiritual value to the kingdom as disciple makers, kingdom builders, sages, servants, and teachers. This segment also tends to have more discretionary time to engage in both apprenticeship learning and training.

At our 2023 Board of Trustees retreat, I presented some of my ideas about engaging and pursuing Christian spiritual elders and witnessed great enthusiasm bubbling inside those who anticipated enthralling possibilities. I had a wonderful opportunity to create a draft proposal of what form some positive actions might take.

Once again, the Holy Spirit spoke up, compelling me to name this ministry, "The Crown of Glory Fellows Ministry!"

As I continued, the next words that entered me were:

The Crown of Glory Fellows Ministry
A collaborative ministry for...

As my proposal began to take shape, I received the annual report from the Colson Center in the mail. The inside cover, in bold print, read, "A Legacy of Collaboration." The articles in that issue highlighted different collaborative efforts between the Colson Center and various Christian groups.

Thank you, Jesus, for endlessly showing me that you always have an even greater plan for us!

During the process, I received great encouragement and multitudes of loving, insightful feedback. One question concerned the ministry "deliverables." I propose two:

1. Intergenerational awakening and revival of the Holy Spirit.
2. Intergenerational making of disciples and disciple makers.

The next phase involves "populating" the process. This will involve select people of God and followers of Jesus continuing to share stories, including disclosing details of our own processes of growing love and surrender to the Lord.

The appendix of this book offers more specific details about the Crown of Glory Fellows Ministry.

The spirit of Jesus in me greets the spirit of Jesus in you and brings us together to the Father and the Son and The Holy Spirit! Amen.

Love you,
Stan Goss

APPENDIX

Crown of Glory Fellows Ministry

A Collaborative, Small Group Ministry

Finishing Well: Making robust spirit-revived and guided life transitions into spiritual eldership, disciple making, and service.

Vision

Because the Kingdom of Heaven is ontologically distinct from the world, the Church Jesus is building must be categorically different. Everywhere you find the Church Jesus is building it will reveal a DNA of inter-generality, unearthing a culture of spiritual parenting and grandparenting.

– J.D. Walt, *Wake Up Call*

Purposes

1. To be transformed by the Holy Spirit within.
2. To come to know Jesus intimately.
3. To become disciple makers and makers of disciple makers.

Resources

Two training manuals:

1. *Life in the Presence of God: Practices for Living in Light of Eternity (IVP, 2017)* by Ken Boa, a training manual for living in the Holy Spirit filled presence of God.
2. *Holy Bible*, the instructional manual for living.

Rationale for the Ministry

I hope I can convince you that becoming more conscious of God's moment-to-moment presence is something that you need and can have. It's an innate capacity that every true follower of Christ has and can cultivate.

From the time a person first believes (is born again), God puts His Holy Spirit in every believer (Pentecost), and that Spirit is now available to us every second of every day. (Romans 8:11; 1 Corinthians e:16; Ephesians 1:13-14)

MOST CHRISTIANS LIVE UNAWARE OF THIS DIVINE PRESENCE, to our own detriment and impoverishment. More than that, we do so at the risk of being disobedient to the commands of Jesus. (John 4:8)

– Excerpt from the "Introduction" to *Life in the Presence of God*

Training

C. S. Lewis said that, as Followers of Christ, we are basically "amphibians." We exist in the natural world and the spiritual world both interchangeably and simultaneously. The way to grow and develop in the spiritual world is through an elaborate process of training.

This ministry includes a rigorous training process. Member participation will help awaken, develop, and nurture an increased Christ-consciousness in everyday living.

"If you put these things before the brothers, you will be a good servant of Christ Jesus, being trained in the words of the faith and of the good doctrine that you have followed. Have nothing to do with irreverent, silly myths. Rather train yourself for godliness; for while bodily training is of some value, godliness is of value in every way, as it holds promise for the present life and also for the life to come." (1 Timothy 4:6-9)

People

Engage in small group training. Call people together, form teams of 6-10 people, select team leaders, name teams (biblical names: e.g., Joshua team, Esther team, etc.), select one person as a training partner, collect team information, and set up team meeting schedules.

The purpose of teams includes the following:

- To foster effective communications and create a life-changing community and brotherhood/sisterhood.
- Do ministry, do not just dole out information.
- There is no substitute for face-to-face, in-person interaction.
- Meet in circles.
- Engage people.
- Multiply.
- Support, encourage, and hold each other accountable.
- Listen, check-in often, even daily, with a partner; weekly within teams; and monthly within larger groups.
- Teams are "open" and can add additional members or split at any time.

Time

Create committed calendars for group gatherings.

- Monthly, for larger groups.
- Weekly, for teams.
- More frequently, for one-on-one with training partners.
- Incorporate periodic phone or online audio/video calls for participants to share stories and enjoy inspiring speakers.

SYLLABUS

Crown of Glory Fellows Ministry

Training Manual: *Life in the Presence of God: Practices for Living in Light of Eternity (IVP, 2017)* by Ken Boa.

Module ONE
Context: Awakening and Revival
Pre-read Chapters 1-4.

Chapter 1: The Secret
The simple secret: The Christian life means *Life in Christ!* None of this happens by human effort alone. All of it requires the help of the Holy Spirit, who lives in every believer. If we want to take this secret and run with it, there are two things that we have to do: The first is "trust," and the second is "train." Note our *"amphibious nature."*

Chapter 2: The Images
"I am the vine; you are the branches...apart from me you can do nothing" (John 15:5). It's a process of becoming who Jesus has already made us. We are only branches. Abide. Stay. Be in. Christ. But when we do, there's joy!

Chapter 3: The Exemplar
We imitate Christ by identifying ourselves with Him. Without the Spirit, we can never live like Jesus, but with it we can. Do you get the sense that Jesus' prayers were not only personal, but almost constant? Do you, like Jesus, talk to God as though He's always there?

Chapter 4: The Walk
"Therefore as you have received Christ Jesus the Lord, so walk in Him." (Colossians 2:6)

Module TWO
Context: Training
Pre-read Chapter 5.

Chapter 5: Training
"Train yourself to be godly" (1 Timothy 4:7). In any form of training, it's one step, one skill, at a time, and then practice, practice, practice. There's a big difference between trying and training, and it's the difference between success and failure in the area of spiritual training.

Module THREE
Context: Retraining
Pre-read Chapter 6.

Chapter 6: Rewiring Your Mind
Our brains are constantly transforming. Intelligence is fluid, not fixed, and our brains have an astounding capacity for growth, even as we grow older. As Christians, we're called to be always growing, drawing nearer to Him, and becoming more like Christ. We're never supposed to plateau, spiritually; never to retire from growth and learning, even in old age (see Psalm 92:12-14). It's feasible to train our minds to be more open to God. We must adapt our thinking to see the world like He sees it. We must reorganize our lives around practices that help us become more aware of His presence.

Module FOUR
Context: Reseeing
Pre-read Chapter 7.

Chapter 7: Re-seeing the World
A new set of eyes, so to speak, will develop within us, enabling us to look at God while our outward eyes watch the scenes of this passing world. According to A. J. Tozer in *The Pursuit of God* (as summarized by Boa in *Life in the Presence of God*), "Will we continue to live in an illusion or embrace our true identity as children of God? To embrace our true identity means we'll have to reverse our worldview and rewire our brains so that we see as God sees." (p. 148)

Module FIVE
Context: Reorganizing
Pre-read Chapter 8.

Chapter 8: Reorganizing Your Time
Perhaps the greatest threat to utilizing any concept from this book is busyness. And though applying these principles may not require a complete overhaul of your schedule, it is going to force a great shift in how you view your time. Christian philosopher and theologian Dallas Willard once privately counseled author and pastor John Ortberg, "Hurry is the great enemy of spiritual life in our day. You must ruthlessly eliminate hurry from your life." (Boa, p. 174)

Module SIX
Context: Rejoicing
Pre-read Chapter 9.

Chapter 9: Rejoicing Amid Suffering

Jesus guaranteed that all will have trouble in this world (see John 16:33). Suffering is no elective, but a required course in the university of life. There's no way around suffering, but there is a way through; with it that helps us. Come out better on the other side, and it's with Him (see Psalm 23: 4-1; 1 Peter 5:10).

Module SEVEN
Context: Repenting
Pre-read Chapter 10.

Chapter 10: Repenting of Sin

Sin can never master a person who has committed his or her life to Christ, no matter how bad it is. "For sin shall no longer be your master, because you are not under the law, but under grace" (Romans 6:14). Also, the sin that hinders your relationship with God isn't even a small part of who you are anymore. You have a new identity, a deepest you, if you are in Christ" (see Hebrews 12:1).

Module EIGHT
Context: Remaining
Pre-read Chapter 11.

Chapter 11: Remaining in Community
We're not solely a bunch of self-contained "temples" of the Holy Spirit, but also one body of believers, living together in His presence, as we will for all eternity. Living in God's presence is something we do together. We need each other to keep living in Him. Soul care includes: 1) Spiritual friendship; 2) Spiritual guidance; 3) Spiritual mentoring; and 4) Spiritual direction.

Module NINE
Context: Reimaging
Pre-read Chapter 12.

Chapter 12: Reimaging Life
Christians live within the context of a great story, a story much bigger than ourselves and with a plot that we know begins and ends well in eternal perfection! But many of us don't yet feel or look like people living that kind of amazing story. The words "eternal perfection" do not sound exciting to us, but rather dull. This is a deficit in our imagination, not in eternity itself.

Tears of Sorrow, Tears of Joy

ABOUT THE AUTHOR

Stan Goss has enjoyed a thirty-year career as a Master Executive Coach, working nationally and internationally with senior leaders in the arenas of Leadership and Leadership Development. He has worked hand-in-hand with CEOs in a wide range of sectors, including Oil and Gas, Banking, Health Care, Retail, Power Generation and Major Universities. Stan is an impassioned, lifelong student of Leadership and Human Behavior.

For the past ten years, Stan has gotten off the travel circuit, which netted him over a million frequent traveler miles. He's turned his focus and time toward watching his ten grandkids flourish in their schools. Additionally, as a proud servant of his world, he has dedicated himself to community service for an area he loves and calls home: Katy, Texas.

As a Board of Governors member of the Katy Area Economic Development Council, Stan headed the Leadership Committee, a dedicated and talented group of volunteers. This group's most noteworthy achievement has been to provide the energy and spark that led to establishing the University of Houston (UH) Katy campus, which is becoming the anchoring branch of a campus which includes UH Victoria and Houston Community College (HCC), ultimately supporting over 20,000 students.

Stan is a lifelong learner, with a B.S. Degree in Public Administration from the University of Denver. He also attended the Colorado School of Mines and Duke University Law School. More recently, he completed eight-semesters to earn a Bible Certificate from The Bible Seminary and completed the nine- month Colson Fellows program. Stan is also blessed to serve on the Board of Trustees of The Bible Seminary.

Stan was blessed to be the first recipient of the "Stan Stanley Eagle Award" for community service in economic development and was named one of the Top 100 Men of Katy by *Katy Magazine.*

Stan, and his wife, Suzi, have been Katy-area residents for more than four decades and have proudly witnessed two generations of children and grandchildren flourish in Katy Independent School District (KISD) schools and beyond in various colleges and careers.

At the time of this book's publication, at the age of 85, Stan is still going strong. He devotes much of his time and energy toward building a ministry that the Lord has placed within his heart, called Crown of Glory Fellows Ministry based on Proverbs 16:31, "Gray hair is a crown of glory. It is the result of a righteous life." Part of a national retirement restoration movement, the ministry is devoted to inspiring and encouraging Christian spiritual eldership.

www.ingramcontent.com/pod-product-compliance
Lightning Source LLC
Chambersburg PA
CBHW060524100426
42743CB00009B/1419